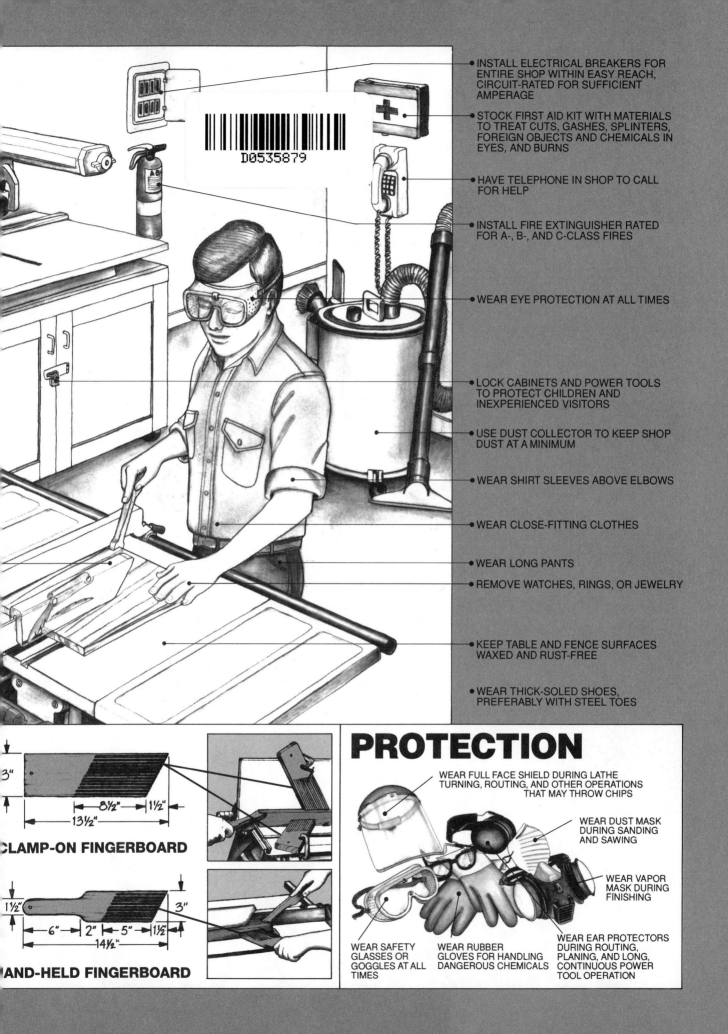

- INSTALL ELECTRICAL BREAKERS FOR ENTIRE SHOP WITHIN EASY REACH, CIRCUIT-RATED FOR SUFFICIENT AMPERAGE
- STOCK FIRST AID KIT WITH MATERIALS TO TREAT CUTS, GASHES, SPLINTERS, FOREIGN OBJECTS AND CHEMICALS IN EYES, AND BURNS
- HAVE TELEPHONE IN SHOP TO CALL FOR HELP
- INSTALL FIRE EXTINGUISHER RATED FOR A-, B-, AND C-CLASS FIRES
- WEAR EYE PROTECTION AT ALL TIMES
- LOCK CABINETS AND POWER TOOLS TO PROTECT CHILDREN AND INEXPERIENCED VISITORS
- USE DUST COLLECTOR TO KEEP SHOP DUST AT A MINIMUM
- WEAR SHIRT SLEEVES ABOVE ELBOWS
- WEAR CLOSE-FITTING CLOTHES
- WEAR LONG PANTS
- REMOVE WATCHES, RINGS, OR JEWELRY
- KEEP TABLE AND FENCE SURFACES WAXED AND RUST-FREE
- WEAR THICK-SOLED SHOES, PREFERABLY WITH STEEL TOES

CLAMP-ON FINGERBOARD

3"
8½" — 1½"
13½"

AND-HELD FINGERBOARD

1½"
6" — 2" — 5" — 1½"
14½"
3"

PROTECTION

WEAR FULL FACE SHIELD DURING LATHE TURNING, ROUTING, AND OTHER OPERATIONS THAT MAY THROW CHIPS

WEAR DUST MASK DURING SANDING AND SAWING

WEAR VAPOR MASK DURING FINISHING

WEAR EAR PROTECTORS DURING ROUTING, PLANING, AND LONG, CONTINUOUS POWER TOOL OPERATION

WEAR RUBBER GLOVES FOR HANDLING DANGEROUS CHEMICALS

WEAR SAFETY GLASSES OR GOGGLES AT ALL TIMES

THE WORKSHOP COMPANION®

USING HAND TOOLS

TECHNIQUES FOR BETTER WOODWORKING

by Nick Engler

Rodale Press
Emmaus, Pennsylvania

Printed in the United States of America on acid-free ∞, recycled ♺ paper

If you have any questions or comments concerning this book, please write:
    Rodale Press
    Book Readers' Service
    33 East Minor Street
    Emmaus, PA 18098

About the Author: Nick Engler is an experienced wood-worker, writer, teacher, and inventor. He worked as a luthier for many years, making traditional American musi-cal instruments before he founded *Hands On!* magazine. He has taught at the University of Cincinnati and gives wood-working seminars around the country. He contributes to woodworking magazines and designs tools for America's Best Tool Company. This is his forty-first book.

Series Editor: Kevin Ireland
Editors: Ken Burton
            Roger Yepsen
Copy Editor: Sarah Dunn
Graphic Designer: Linda Watts
Illustrator: Mary Jane Favorite
Master Craftsman: Jim McCann
Photographer: Karen Callahan
Cover Photographer: Mitch Mandel
Proofreader: Hue Park
Indexer: Beverly Bremer
Interior and endpaper illustrations by Mary Jane Favorite
Produced by Bookworks, Inc., West Milton, Ohio

Special Thanks to:

Robertson's Cabinets, Inc.
West Milton, Ohio

George F. Vander Voort
Carpenter Technology Corporation
Reading, Pennsylvania

Garrett Wade
New York, New York

Wertz Hardware
West Milton, Ohio

Library of Congress Cataloging-in-Publication Data

Engler, Nick.
    Using hand tools/by Nick Engler
        p.   cm. — (The workshop companion)
    Includes index.
    ISBN 0–87596–680–2 hardcover
    1. Woodworking tools. I. Title.
    II. Series: Engler, Nick. Workshop companion.
TT186.E526   1995
684 '.082 — dc20   94–25297
                                            CIP

2 4 6 8 10 9 7 5 3 1 hardcover

CONTENTS

TECHNIQUES

PROJECTS

TECHNIQUES

1

WHY USE HAND TOOLS?

Woodworkers have been arguing the relative merits of hand and machine work since power tools first appeared nearly 200 years ago. Some prefer power tools for their precision and the time they save; others champion hand tools because they bring craftsmen into intimate contact with their materials.

Gustav Stickley, one of America's most accomplished craftsmen, advocated another view — one that emphasized neither hand nor power tools. Stickley designed furniture at the beginning of the 1900s and was the patron saint of the American Arts and Crafts movement. Elsewhere in the world, the Arts and Crafts philosophy was a reaction against the Industrial Revolution, particularly the factory system and the use of woodworking machines. Writing in his *Craftsman* magazine, Stickley defended power tools, saying they could do a better job in many tasks, especially preparing the wood and cutting it to size. But he did not reject handwork. He advised craftsmen that their overriding concern must be the beauty and utility of their furniture, not how it's built. They should use whatever tools work best for them.

THE HAND TOOL ADVANTAGE

POWER TOOLS WON'T DO EVERYTHING

If, as Stickley asserted, you can build better furniture with machines, why use hand tools at all?

Because you can't do everything with power tools. A few tasks, like measuring, have not yet been automated. Others are only partly automated. For example, if you want to cut a mortise with a router, you must either square the ends of the mortise with a chisel or round the top and bottom of the tenon with a file — the technique requires *some* handwork. And there are other tasks, like scraping a wood surface smooth, that you can do better with hand tools. (*See Figure 1-1.*)

If you work only with power tools, you limit yourself and your woodworking. Your projects are confined to just what the machines can do. But if you know how to use hand *and* power tools, you increase your options. You have more woodworking techniques to choose from so you can tackle a broader range of projects.

1-1 There isn't a power sander made that cuts as quickly or smoothly as a properly sharpened cabinet scraper. With just a few strokes, you can scrape a wood surface as smooth as you could sand it by working your way up to 150-grit sandpaper.

A DIFFERENT LOOK AND FEEL

One way in which hand tools expand your woodworking horizons is by producing a different surface. Most power tools cut with a rotary motion, scooping the wood and leaving mill marks. In contrast, hand tools cut in a straight line. The marks are often more subtle, and they are always irregular in spacing and height. (*See Figure 1-2.*)

1-2 Power cutting tools and hand cutting tools leave very different surfaces on the wood. Most power tools cut with a rotary motion, scooping the wood as you feed the work. This leaves regular ridges or *mill marks.* Hand tools cut by shearing the wood in a straight line. Provided the cutter is sharp, it leaves few marks; the surface is almost perfectly level. And if you examine a machine-cut surface with a microscope, you'll find a rotary cutter often tears or crushes the cells on the surface — not because of the motion itself, but because the cutting angle is fairly high. There is much less cellular damage with a sharp hand tool because the cutting angles are usually lower.

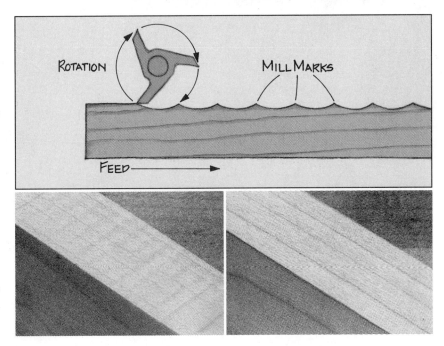

These irregularities blend into the surface when the wood is sanded and finished, just as mill marks do, but minute evidences of them remain. Some say that the wood has a "softer" look and feel or that it takes a finish differently.

HIGH-TECH HAND TOOLS

As you learn to work with hand tools, you'll find they are sophisticated machines with surprising capabilities. The common misconception is that hand tools are an inferior technology, and that by using them you are doing things the "old way."

In fact, most of the hand tools in common use today are the products of modern engineering. Some, like the tape measure and the Surform rasp, are fairly recent inventions. (*See Figure 1-3.*) Even tools that have been around for centuries, like the chisel, have been refined for contemporary craftsmen. The design and materials that go into today's chisels are vastly superior to what was available to an eighteenth-century woodworker.

So when you use hand tools, you're likely using a product of contemporary minds. And the techniques required to use them are contemporary as well — you are doing things the modern way.

A PARTING THOUGHT

Very soon, you will have a *third* choice. You will be able to work wood by hand, machine, and *computer.*

Computer Numerically Controlled (CNC) routers, lathes, saws, and drills are becoming commonplace — metalworking hobbyists have been using them for years. And the prices of CNC woodworking machines are coming down; soon they'll be within the means of home craftsmen. (*See Figure 1-4.*) It's not hard to foresee a time when woodworkers will ask what is the sense in learning to set up old-fashioned power tools when computer-driven routers and laser saws are so much faster and more accurate.

But even as CNC tools take over a larger share of the market, manufacturers of hand and power tools will take advantage of new technologies and new designs. And there will be new techniques for using these improved tools. Woodworking, despite its long history, is a modern craft in constant flux. The tools and techniques (hand, power, and computer) will evolve and remain useful.

As Stickley advised, take advantage of the entire spectrum of tools that are available to you. To be the best craftsman you can be, don't learn just part of the craft.

1-3 Easy to use, effective, and versatile, the Surform is the product of twentieth-century technology. Interchangeable cutting surfaces allow you to use this hand tool as a scrub plane, trimmer, scorp, hollow plane, and rasp.

1-4 Computer Numerically Controlled (CNC) tools, such as this router, are run by a computer. Using a drafting program, you draw the part you want to cut on the computer screen. The computer then sends instructions to small servo motors that move the router back and forth, side to side, and up and down, cutting a precise copy of what you have drawn.

2

MEASURING AND MARKING

While almost every other phase of woodworking has become automated to some degree, measuring and marking are still done mainly by eye, and for good reason — the eye is an extremely accurate measuring instrument. Consider this: After two centuries of training soldiers to shoot, the U.S. Army knows that all but the worst marksmen can hit a target 1 foot in diameter from 100 feet away. In this situation, the human eye, aided only by the sight on the rifle barrel, is accurate to within one-quarter of one degree. And most people do much better than that!

It is not difficult for any craftsman to measure accurately to one-quarter of a degree or one-hundredth of an inch. With the right measuring tools, you can easily see increments this small. The trick is knowing which tools to use and how to read them.

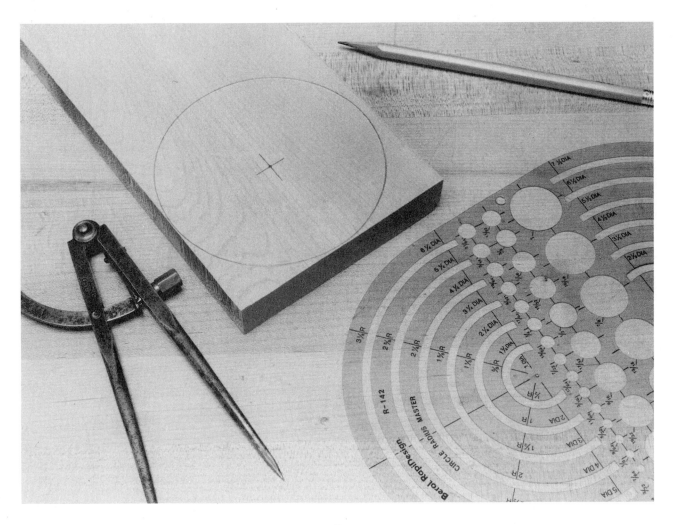

MEASURING TOOLS

LINEAR MEASURE

Most of the measurements you make in your shop are *linear,* such as measuring the length or width of a board. The two most commonly used tools for this task are the *ruler* and the *tape measure.* Rulers are most often used for measuring short distances, under 12 inches, while tape measures gauge longer dimensions, up to the length of the tape. Other common linear measuring tools include both wood and metal *folding rules. (SEE FIGURE 2-1.)*

When purchasing a ruler, look for markings in ¹⁄₆₄- and ¹⁄₃₂-inch graduations. These are the smallest increments that you will use in normal woodworking. (Many shop rulers have an English scale on one side and a metric scale on the other.) Also look for a *thin* ruler or one with a beveled edge. Both bring the scale closer to the object that you are measuring, making it easier to measure accurately. Tape measures are already quite thin and usually come with ¹⁄₃₂- and ¹⁄₁₆-inch graduations. *(SEE FIGURES 2-2 AND 2-3.)*

The hook on the tip of a tape measure is supposed to be loose; it's designed to move the width of the metal tab for accuracy when making both inside and outside measurements. Don't let the tape snap into case — this will elongate the tab's rivet holes and make outside measurements inaccurate. Eventually, it will weaken the tip and the hook will break off.

Use just one tape measure and one ruler around your shop. There are often slight differences from one measuring device to another, and if you use several of them interchangeably, your measurements won't be consistent. Also, the fewer linear measuring tools you have, the easier it is to keep them calibrated to one another. To calibrate a tape measure to a ruler, first measure a short distance (about 6 inches) from the end of a board using the ruler. Then gauge the same distance with the tape measure. If the two distances differ, bend the hook on the tape measure slightly until they're exactly the same.

2-1 *Rulers* (1) come in many different lengths, but the sizes preferred by most craftsmen are 6 and 12 inches. You may also find 24- and 36-inch rulers useful, but they are awkward to handle when measuring small distances. A *tape measure* (2) is handy for longer measurements; you can unroll as much of the tape as you need. Get one with a locking mechanism to prevent the tape from retracting into its case until you are finished measuring. A *folding ruler* (3) is used for both long and short measurements — you unfold only as much of the ruler as you need.

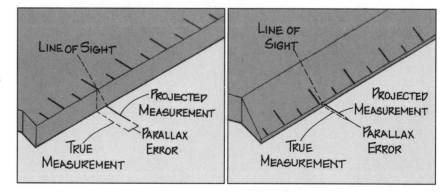

2-2 When you sight a ruler from an angle, you get a *diagonal error* — your eye projects the line on the scale to a position on the wood's surface slightly beyond it, a phenomenon known as parallax. For this reason, always read a ruler from directly overhead. Also, use a *thin* ruler or one with a beveled edge. The closer the graduations are to the object being measured, the smaller the amount of diagonal error.

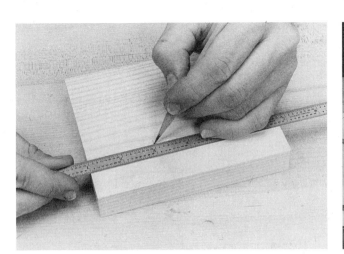

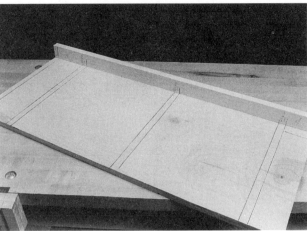

2-3 When using a ruler or tape measure, it's good practice to measure from one line on the scale to another. For example, when measuring 2 inches from the edge of a board, align the 1-inch line on the scale with the edge and make your mark at 3 inches (3 – 1 = 2). If possible, don't start measuring with the end of the scale. Because the ends of a ruler get beat up, they are not especially accurate "0" references. Also, most people sight the end of a ruler differently than they sight the lines. This may introduce a small amount of error into your measurement.

2-4 A *storystick* is a shopmade scale used to make specific measurements on a project. For example, when building a set of cabinets, you must mark the joinery in the cabinet sides the same on every piece. Cut a stick the length of the side, measure and mark the positions of the dadoes and rabbets on the stick, then use that storystick to measure and mark the cabinet sides. This not only speeds up the task of laying out the joinery in the cabinet sides, it also reduces the risk of mismeasuring a dado or a rabbet.

TRY THIS TRICK

Use headband magnifiers, a loupe, or a magnifying lamp to help read 1/32- and 1/64-inch scales accurately, especially when doing layout work. Laying out a part or a joint often involves many exacting measurements. This can be hard on the unaided eye, even with good eyesight.

In addition to rulers and tapes with standardized scales, you may want to invent your own scales for certain projects. A *storystick* can be just as accurate as a commercial scale, especially when you must make repetitive measurements. (*See Figure* 2-4.)

MEASURING ANGLES

In addition to measuring distances when woodworking, you must also measure angles. The angle that you must measure most often is 90 degrees, and for this you need a precision *square.* (*See Figure* 2-5.)

Don't skimp on this tool; purchase as good a square as you can afford. There are several types:

■ A *try square* measures inside and outside corners. The base is thicker than the blade and provides a shoulder that you can butt up against a board, automatically squaring the blade to the edge.

■ An *engineer's square* is a small try square, especially useful for layout work and machine setups.

■ A *double square* has a sliding blade with a scale printed on it.

■ A *carpenter's square* is usually larger than a try square and can be useful for checking assemblies and large setups. Unlike other squares, it has no base or shoulder. Instead, it has two blades — one long and one short — with scales printed on both.

For laying out and setting up miter joints, use a *miter square* to measure 45- and 135-degree angles. Or purchase a *combination square,* a tool that measures 45-, 90-, and 135-degree angles. It can also be used as a ruler, a level, a depth gauge, and a marking tool. Many woodworkers use a combination square almost exclusively instead of keeping an assortment of squares at hand. (*SEE FIGURE 2-6.*)

Typically, there is a bubble level and an awl in the head so you can also use the square as a level and a marking tool. (The awl is too small to be used comfortably, but it's there in case you don't have anything better on hand.) **Note:** Combination squares come in different sizes, from 4 to 24 inches.

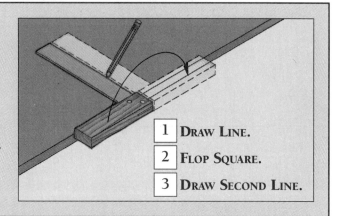

FOR BEST RESULTS

Test a square before you use it, making sure it measures a precise 90 degrees. Joint an edge of a board straight and butt either the base or the head of the square against it. Using the blade as a straightedge, scribe a line perpendicular to the board's edge. Turn the square over so the base points in the opposite direction and scribe a second line next to the first. The two lines must be parallel — if they aren't, the square isn't square.

1	**DRAW LINE.**
2	**FLOP SQUARE.**
3	**DRAW SECOND LINE.**

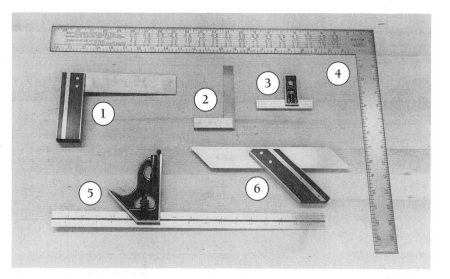

2-5 There are many different types of squares, but the most common are the *try square* (1), the *engineer's square* (2), the *double square* (3), and the *carpenter's square* (4). All of these measure 90-degree angles. The *combination square* (5) will measure 45, 90, and 135 degrees, while the *miter square* (6) measures 45 and 135 degrees .

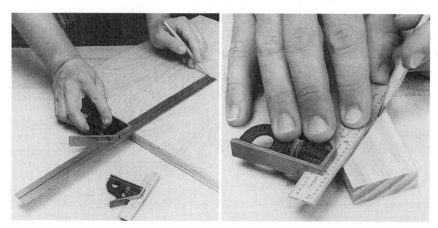

2-6 Of all the squares available, the combination square is the most popular, and with good reason. It performs a number of common measuring and marking tasks, eliminating the need to keep an assortment of tools on hand. In addition to measuring 45-, 90-, and 135-degree angles, the blade serves as a ruler and a straightedge. The head of the square slides along the blade, making a serviceable depth gauge and marking gauge.

You can also use *steel triangles* to measure various angles. These are right triangles — one corner is 90 degrees and the others are either 30, 45, or 60 degrees, depending on the design of the triangle. (*See* *Figure* 2-7.)

To measure angles between 0 and 180 degrees that are not necessarily divisible by 45 degrees, use a *steel protractor.* Get one with a square head; these are more versatile than the round-head types. A *protractor head* for a combination square also measures angles from 0 to 180 degrees. It's larger than a protractor and won't work in tight spaces, but it has broader shoulders and is more stable. You can duplicate and transfer angles with a *sliding T-bevel*. This tool doesn't actually measure an angle; it simply copies it, enabling you to

mark the angle on a surface or use it in setting up a machine. If you must know the number of degrees, use the sliding T-bevel in combination with a protractor. (*See* *Figure* 2-8.)

THICKNESS AND DIAMETER

Although you can measure the thickness of a board or the diameter of a cylinder with a ruler, it's much easier and usually more accurate to use a *caliper*. There are two common types:

■ A *steel caliper* consists of two metal jaws that act as "feeler gauges" for inside and outside measurements. It doesn't actually measure thickness and diameter; it simply transfers or copies a dimension.

2-7 A set of *steel triangles* is handy for layout work and tool setups. A set normally consists of a 45/90 triangle and a 30/60/90 triangle, letting you measure 30, 45, 60, and 90 degrees. They are available in different sizes and often have other layout aids stamped in the interior. Some of these large metal triangles have circle templates cut into their interiors.

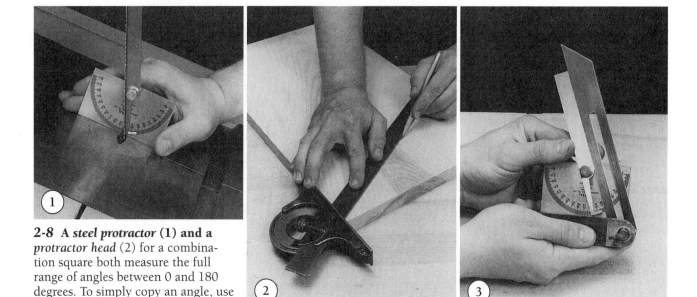

2-8 A *steel protractor* (1) and a *protractor head* (2) for a combination square both measure the full range of angles between 0 and 180 degrees. To simply copy an angle, use a *sliding T-bevel* (3).

It is most often used in lathe turning to tell the craftsman when the turning has arrived at a specific diameter. (SEE FIGURE 2-9.)

■ A *sliding caliper* measures inside and outside dimensions up to 6 inches between a sliding jaw and a fixed jaw. Most have a probe to measure depth as well. Depending on the design of the tool, you can read the measurement on either a scale or a dial indicator. It is extremely precise and is especially helpful when planing wood and cutting joinery. (SEE FIGURE 2-10.)

TRY THIS TRICK

Use an open-end wrench as a fixed caliper for measuring small dimensions, such as the diameters of round tenons or the thickness of planed wood. The distance between the jaws is equal to the size of the wrench, plus .010 inch.

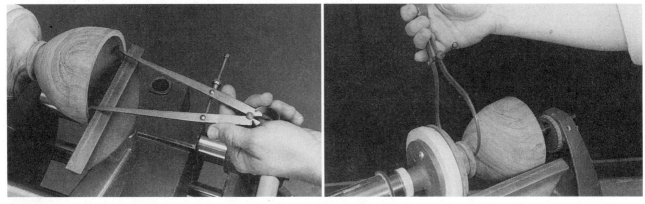

2-9 A *steel caliper* transfers or copies a measurement. There are two types of calipers available — one for outside dimensions and the other for inside dimensions. To use the caliper, you must first set the jaws to the desired dimension, measuring the distance between the tips of the jaws with a ruler or a tape measure. Then hold the caliper lightly against the object you wish to measure. When the jaws slip over the object (or inside it), the object is the proper size.

2-10 A *slide caliper* is capable of both inside and outside measurements. It can also be used as a depth gauge. It is extremely accurate — a well-made slide caliper with a scale on its side can measure in increments as small as $\frac{1}{128}$ inch. A slide caliper with a dial indicator — often called a *dial caliper* — will measure to $\frac{1}{1000}$ inch. Most have a 6-inch capacity.

MEASURING FLUSH, FLAT, AND LEVEL

Next to a square, the most important measuring tool in your shop is a precision *straightedge* — a length of steel with one or both edges machined to be perfectly flat. These are a necessity for properly aligning and adjusting tools, for setup and layout, and for checking the straightness of an edge and the flatness of a surface. Once again, don't skimp; get a good one. (*See Figure 2-11.*)

A BIT OF ADVICE

As important as a good straightedge is, it is not as easy to find as a good square. If you can't find a precision straightedge at a reasonable price, have a machinist make one for you from a scrap of steel.

To test the flatness of large surfaces or the straightness of a long edge, use *mason's cord.* (*See Figure 2-12.*) Pull the cord taut to make it perfectly straight. Unlike ordinary string, this cord won't sag or stretch.

You occasionally must make sure surfaces are horizontal, as well as flat and straight. For this, you need a level. You can make do with the level in your combination square or use an ordinary *carpenter's level,* but if you invest in a precision *bench level,* you can also use it as a square and a straightedge. (*See Figure 2-13.*)

In addition to these commercial tools, you may also wish to keep a couple of straight, slender sticks on hand to use as *winding sticks.* These are useful for checking drawers, boxes, and cases to make sure the assemblies are not twisted or *winded.* (*See Figure 2-14.*)

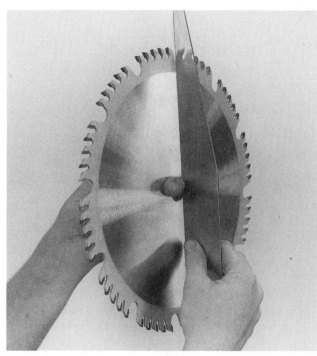

2-11 Some experienced craftsmen claim that the first tool you should buy before *anything* else is a precision straightedge. Use this tool to check and align the tools you buy thereafter — hand planes, saw blades, jointers, and so on. Most woodworking tools have surfaces that must be straight or flat to operate properly, and a straightedge will tell you how straight or flat they are.

2-12 *Mason's cord* makes a super- long straightedge. Just stretch it taut over the surface you want to test; the material will not sag or stretch like ordinary string. It's useful for a wide range of woodworking tasks, from checking how flat or straight a board might be to aligning built-in cabinets as you install them.

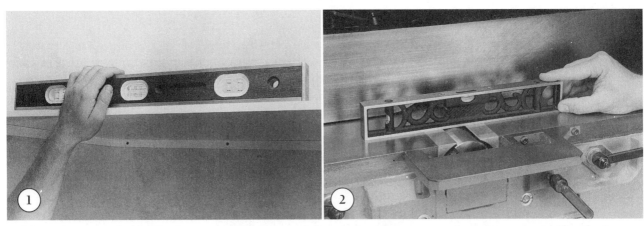

2-13 A *carpenter's level* (1) is relatively inexpensive but makes an excellent tool for leveling surfaces and installing shelves and cabinets. A *bench level* (2) is more expensive, but all the surfaces are machined flat and square to one another, letting you use it as a level, a square, and a straightedge.

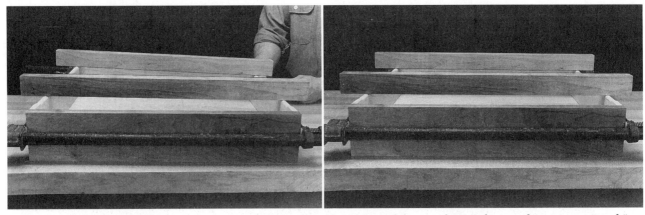

2-14 To use a pair of *winding* sticks, simply lay them across the assembly you want to check, placing one stick near one side and the other near the opposite side. Then sight across them. If the sticks appear parallel, the assembly is flat. If not, the assembly is winded. **Note:** To make the winding sticks easier to "read," cut them from two contrasting colors of wood.

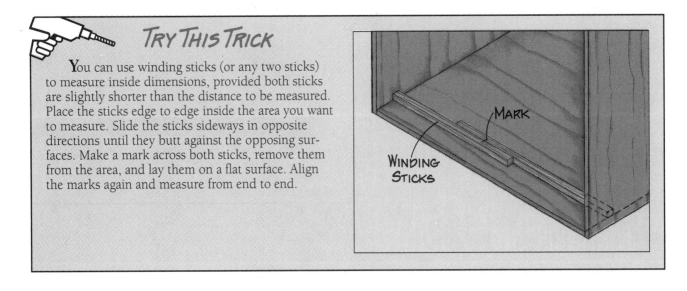

TRY THIS TRICK

You can use winding sticks (or any two sticks) to measure inside dimensions, provided both sticks are slightly shorter than the distance to be measured. Place the sticks edge to edge inside the area you want to measure. Slide the sticks sideways in opposite directions until they butt against the opposing surfaces. Make a mark across both sticks, remove them from the area, and lay them on a flat surface. Align the marks again and measure from end to end.

MARK

WINDING STICKS

SHOP MATH

To work wood, you must know a little math. Before you can cut a board to the proper size and angle, you must be able to read a ruler and a protractor. To join one board to another, you must know how to add and subtract fractions and degrees.

Beyond those basic skills, there are several useful formulas — mathematical shortcuts — that expand your woodworking abilities and increase your precision. These are sometimes lumped together under the imposing heading *shop math*. Don't let the term intimidate you even if you list yourself among the ranks of the Mathematically Challenged. You don't have to be a mathematician or an engineer to take advantage of shop math, you just have to know how to apply the formulas.

Most shop math is derived from a branch of geometry that has to do with *right triangles*. In *trigonometry* (as the branch is called), each right triangle has three parts — a *side* (a), a *base* (b), and a *hypotenuse* (c) — and the angle between the side and the base is always 90 degrees. The angles are usually labeled in capital letters, A, B, and C, according to which part of the triangle is across from them. The right angle is angle C because it's opposite hypotenuse c.

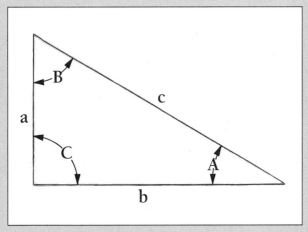

There is an exact proportional relationship between the parts of a right triangle, and it's this relationship that governs shop math: The square of hypotenuse c is equal to the sum of the squares of side a and base b:

$$c^2 = a^2 + b^2$$

This is known as the Pythagorean Theorem, after the Greek philosopher Pythagoras (circa 500 B.C.), who first formulated it. However, the theorem was in use long before Pythagoras. Quite possibly, it's as old as woodworking itself. Early Egyptian carpenters used knotted cords that they stretched into triangles with 3, 4, and 5 equally spaced knots to a side (the same basic relationship that Pythagoras conceived) to lay out right angles.

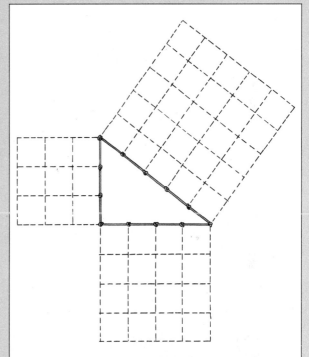

Contemporary craftsmen rarely need this theorem to produce right angles — we have squares for that, another Greek innovation — but it has dozens of other uses. Often, you can divide the design of a project into triangles to help figure missing dimensions. Any rectangular wooden piece, for example, can be divided into two right triangles. Applying the theorem, you can calculate the precise dimension of any part of a right triangle, provided you know the length of the other two parts.

There is also a proportional relationship between the parts of a right triangle and the *angles* at the corners. Using equations derived from the

(continued) ▷

SHOP MATH — CONTINUED

Pythagorean Theorem, mathematicians have assigned each degree between 0 and 90 four proportional values — a *sine, cosine, tangent,* and *cotangent.* (These are usually abbreviated *sin, cos, tan,* and *cot.*) It's not important that you understand how these values are figured. You only need to know that you can use them to find any dimension or any angle in a right triangle, provided you know either the length of two parts or the length of one part and the angle of one corner other than the right (90-degree) corner.

All of the formulas needed to find the dimensions or the angles in a right triangle can be organized into the chart below.

In addition to dividing rectangles into right triangles, you can also scribe right triangles inside *circles.* This helps you figure the dimensions or the radius of curved parts in a project, such as the rocker on a rocking chair. Here are the formulas:

$$r = (l^2 + 4h^2) \div 8h$$

$$h = r - (\sqrt{4r^2 - l^2}) \div 2$$

$$l = 2\sqrt{h(2r - h)}$$

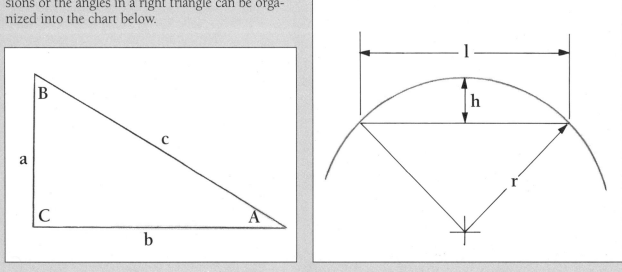

PARTS AND ANGLES KNOWN	FORMULAS FOR PARTS AND ANGLES TO BE FOUND		
Side a, base b	$c = \sqrt{a^2 + b^2}$	$tanA = a \div b$	$B = 90° - A$
Side a, hypotenuse c	$b = \sqrt{c^2 - a^2}$	$sinA = a \div c$	$B = 90° - A$
Base b, hypotenuse c	$a = \sqrt{c^2 - b^2}$	$sinB = b \div c$	$A = 90° - B$
Side a, Angle A	$c = a \div sinA$	$b = a \times cotA$	$B = 90° - A$
Side a, Angle B	$c = a \div cosB$	$b = a \times tanB$	$A = 90° - B$
Base b, Angle A	$c = b \div cosA$	$a = b \times tanA$	$B = 90° - A$
Base b, Angle B	$c = b \div sinB$	$a = b \times cotB$	$A = 90° - B$
Hypotenuse c, angle A	$b = c \times cosA$	$a = c \times sinA$	$B = 90° - A$
Hypotenuse c, angle B	$b = c \times sinB$	$a = c \times cosB$	$A = 90° - B$

To use most of these formulas, you must be able to figure square roots or look up the sines, cosines, tangents, and cotangents of various angles. Tables of these values, as well as instructions for calculating square roots, can be found in most trigonometry and algebra books. However, an inexpensive *scientific* calculator will do all of this for you with a lot less trouble.

Scientific calculators have an array of mysterious keys either above or to one side of the ordinary numerical keypad. Several of these come in handy in shop math. For example, to quickly calculate the square root of a number, enter the number on the numerical keypad, then push the "√" key.

To find the sine, cosine, or tangent value of a degree between 0 and 90, enter the degree on the numerical keypad, then push the appropriate *sin*, *cos*, or *tan* key. To find the degree that corresponds to a sine, cosine, or tangent value, punch the value on the numerical keypad, press the INV or SHIFT key, then the appropriate *sin*, *cos*, or *tan* key. **Note:** There is no cotangent (*cot*) key on most inexpensive scientific calculators. To figure a cotangent, simply divide 1 by the tangent.

As an added bonus, a scientific calculator will also add, subtract, multiply, and divide *fractions* for you, enabling you to figure dimensions in fractions of inches. To enter a fraction, use the key marked "a b/c" or "a/b." **Note:** Exactly how you use this key will depend on the calculator — read your owner's manual.

MARKING TOOLS

POINTS AND LINES

The most frequently used marking device in wood-working is a pencil. It's inexpensive, easy to use, easy to see, and — unfortunately — not especially accurate. A pencil's point dulls easily, becoming broader as you use it. This, in turn, makes it increasingly hard to be accurate. If you lay out a line that grows wider as it progresses down the length of the board, how do you follow the line as you cut?

If you use a pencil to mark wood, there are several things you can do to make the marks more accurate:

■ Use a pencil with a hard lead, such as 3. The marks will be lighter and harder to see, but the point won't dull as quickly.

■ Roll the pencil in your fingers as you use it. The graphite wears in a cone shape and the point remains sharp. (*SEE FIGURE 2-15.*)

■ Use a mechanical .5mm pencil. The point and the lines you draw will always be consistent in width.

The other solution is to avoid using a pencil at all. Many experienced craftsmen advocate *metal* marking tools, especially for layouts where accuracy is critical. The lines left by metal tools are harder to see than pencil marks, but because the points remain sharp, the lines are always crisp and thin.

There are several types of metal marking tools, and they all fall into one of two categories — *blades* and *points*. Blades cut the wood as they mark it; points scratch it. A *marking knife* has a blade designed specifically for marking wood, but you can also use a bench knife, pocket knife, or utility knife. An *awl* has a thin, tapered point for scratching. A *striking knife* provides both a blade and a point. (*SEE FIGURES 2-16 AND 2-17.*)

Blades are usually recommended for marking cross grain, points for marking with the grain. However, this is not a hard-and-fast rule. Use whichever one makes a precise mark that you can follow easily.

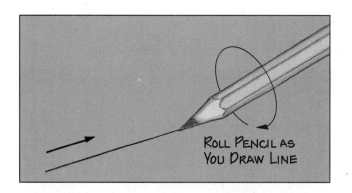

2-15 **If you use a pencil to mark** wood, roll the pencil between your fingers as you draw the line. The graphite wears in a cone shape, the point stays sharp, and the line remains crisp and thin. This makes it easier to follow the line accurately.

ROLL PENCIL AS YOU DRAW LINE

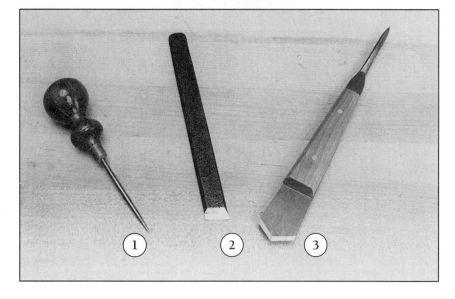

2-16 **Many craftsmen prefer to** work with metal marking tools because they stay sharp and leave a crisp line to follow. An *awl* (1) is a pointed tool used to scratch the wood along the grain. A *marking knife* (2) cuts the wood across the grain. A *striking knife* (3) provides a point for scratching and a blade for cutting.

When laying out extremely long lines when accuracy is not a concern, use a *snap line*. Stretch the chalk-impregnated string over the material, then pluck the cord and let it snap so it leaves a line of chalk dust on the surface. Remember to use blue chalk to avoid staining the wood.

To mark lines parallel to an edge or an end — as when laying out a mortise-and-tenon joint — use a *marking gauge* or a *cutting gauge*. Like an awl, a marking gauge scratches a line with a metal point (called a *spur*), while a cutting gauge uses a small blade, similar to a marking knife. (*See Figure 2-18.*) A *mortising gauge* has two spurs (one fixed, one adjustable) to draw two lines at once. This allows you to mark both sides of a mortise or both cheeks of a tenon in one step. (*See Figure 2-19.*) Some tools combine a marking gauge on one side of the beam and a mortising gauge on the other.

Some woodworking texts advise you to regrind the point on a marking gauge to make a small elliptical blade, essentially making a cutting gauge out of a marking gauge. This is extra work you may not need to do. If a cutting gauge is what you want, purchase a cutting gauge.

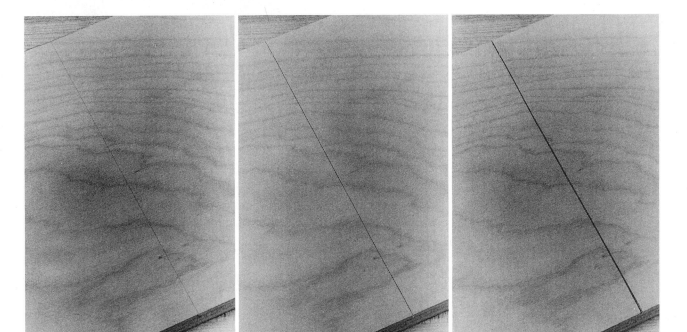

2-17 You may have trouble seeing the lines left by marking blades and points under ordinary shop lighting (left). If so, there are two simple tricks you can try. First, position a light to shine *obliquely* across the wood surface. This will cast shadows, making the lines appear darker (middle).

Second, you can dust the wood surface with the powdered chalk used for snap lines. The chalk will accumulate in the cuts or scratches, making them stand out (right). Use *blue* chalk; red chalk stains wood and will interfere with your finish.

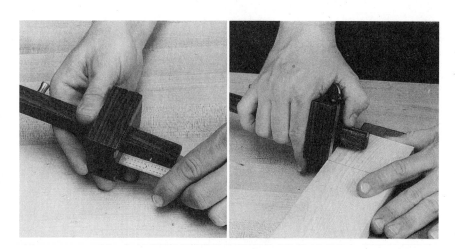

2-18 To use a *marking gauge* or a *cutting gauge*, loosen the locking screw and slide the face along the beam until it's the desired distance from the spur or the blade. Lock the face in place and use it to guide the beam along the edge of the board as you scribe a line parallel to the edge. Traditionally, these tools are pushed rather than pulled, but this is not carved in stone. Use whatever feels comfortable.

2-19 A *mortising gauge* is used in much the same way as a marking gauge, but it has two spurs and draws two parallel lines at once. To use it, first set the distance between the face and the fixed spur, then adjust the gap between the fixed and adjustable spurs. The locking screw that holds the face in place on the beam usually holds the adjustable spur as well.

CIRCLES AND CENTERS

When you need to draw a small circle on a wooden surface, use a *circle template*, a *compass*, or *dividers*. You must use a pencil or pencil lead to mark a circle with a template or a compass, while dividers scratch a line with a metal point. (*See Figure 2-20.*) To make large circles, use *trammel points* — metal scribes that mount to a wooden beam. Some trammel points will hold either a metal point or a pencil. (*See Figure 2-21.*)

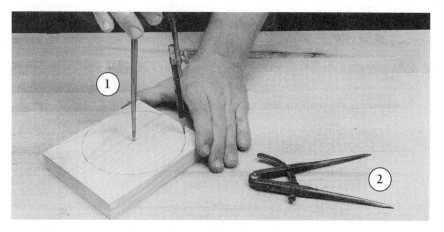

2-20 To mark a circle with a *compass* (1), set the distance between the point and the pencil to the desired radius of the circle, then swing the pencil around the point. The procedure is almost exactly the same with *dividers* (2), but you swing one point around the other, scratching the circle in the surface. Some craftsmen prefer to regrind one of the divider points to make a small blade that cuts the circle.

To find the center of a circular object, such as a lathe turning, use a *center head* or a *center finder.* A center head is an accessory for a combination square. It mounts on the blade like the protractor head mentioned earlier. A center finder is a dedicated tool that performs the same function. (*See Figures* 2-22 *and* 2-23.)

2-21 Use *trammel points* to mark large circles and curves. Mount the trammels on a wooden beam so the distance between them is equal to the radius of the circle you wish to draw. Then swing one trammel around the other.

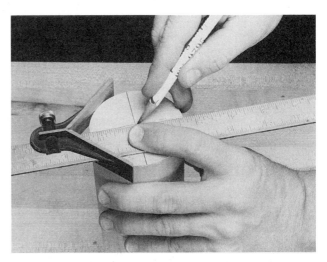

2-22 To use a center head to find the center of a circle, hold the head against the edge of the disc or the cylinder so both arms touch the circumference. Using the blade as a straightedge, mark a line across the diameter of the circle. Turn the center head partway around the circle — it doesn't matter how far — and draw another line. The point where the two lines cross is the center of the circle.

CENTER ARM

¾" (Typ)

6"

6"

6"

90°

45°

OUTSIDE ARMS

½" (Typ)

TOP VIEW

EXPLODED VIEW

CENTER FINDER

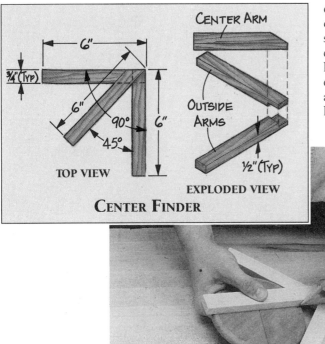

2-23 If you don't have a center head, you can easily make your own center finder. Join two small boards with end laps to make a square. Glue a third board between them so one edge cuts across both the inside and outside corner where the first two boards lap. This edge must be exactly 45 degrees from both boards. Use this edge as a straightedge when locating the center of a circle.

CONTOURS AND COMPLEX SHAPES

To lay out elliptical curves and contours, use *french curves* or a *flexible curve*. French curves are drafting templates that provide a wide range of concave and convex curves. A flexible curve can be adjusted to the curve or contour you need. (*SEE FIGURE 2-24.*)

Copy a curve or a contour with a *contour gauge*. Press the gauge against an object so it conforms to the shape, then use the gauge to trace the shape on another surface. (*SEE FIGURE 2-25.*) To transfer a paper pattern to a wood surface, you have a choice of several simple tools and techniques — use carbon

paper or a pounce wheel, make a photocopy and iron it, or make a template. (*SEE FIGURE 2-26.*) If you must enlarge or reduce the pattern, use a *pantograph*. (*SEE FIGURE 2-27.*)

> ### TRY THIS TRICK
> Use a photocopier with enlarging and reducing capabilities to size a pattern. Most copying services have these machines.

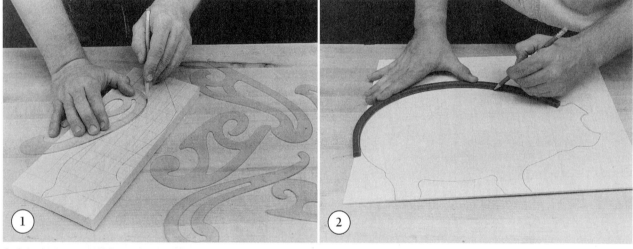

2-24 Use a set of *french curves* (1) to guide a pencil when drawing elliptical curves and contours. Each of these drafting tools has several different concave and convex curves to choose from. Experiment with them until you find the shapes you need for your layout. Or, use a *flexible curve* (2) and simply bend it to the shape you need.

2-25 A *contour gauge* (also called a *profile gauge*) copies or transfers shapes and contours. It's made up of several hundred metal pins or plastic blades mounted on a bar so they all slide independently. To copy a shape, place one side of the gauge against the object. Press in gently until the ends of the pins all contact the surface. One side of the gauge will assume a *negative* of the shape, the other side, a *positive*.

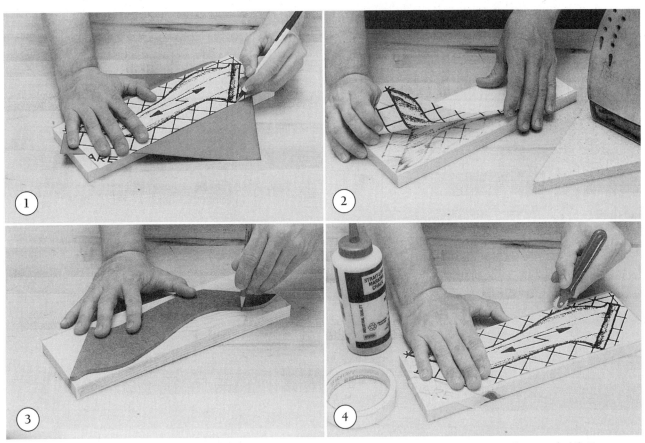

2-26 There are several tools and techniques you can use to transfer a paper pattern to a wood surface: (1) Place carbon paper between the pattern and the wood, then trace the pattern with a ballpoint pen or a stylus. (2) Make a photocopy of the pattern, tape the photocopy to the wood surface with the pattern face down, and rub it with a dry, hot iron. The heat will transfer the pattern from the paper to the wood; however, the image will be *reversed*. (3) Fasten the pattern to a piece of posterboard or hardboard with spray adhesive, then cut the pattern with a scroll saw, band saw, or coping saw. Use this as a template to trace the pattern onto the wood. (4) Tape the pattern to the wood surface and trace it with a *pounce wheel*. This tool leaves small indentations in the wood. Remove the paper pattern and dust the wood surface with blue chalk. The chalk will collect in the indentations, making the pattern easier to see.

2-27 A *pantograph* is a drafting tool that will enlarge or reduce two-dimensional shapes and patterns. It looks like a flexible parallelogram with pivots at each corner. There is a stylus attached to one corner and a pencil mounted at the end of an arm. As you trace the pattern with the stylus, the pencil draws an enlarged or reduced copy. You control the percentage of the enlargement or reduction by adjusting the positions of the pivots. Pantographs are available at most art supply stores and through some woodworking catalogs.

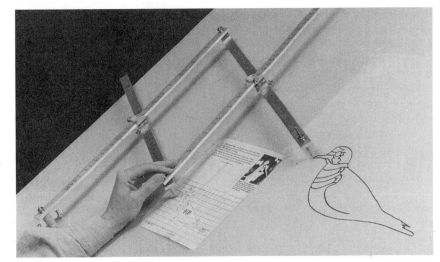

DRAWING AN OVAL

While a circle has a single pivot, or *center*, an oval has two pivots, or *focii*. To draw an oval, you must swing a pencil around these focii just as you swing a pencil around a center to make a circle. The trick is locating the focii. To do this, you must first decide how long and how wide you want to make the oval. The length of the oval is its *major axis*, and the width is its *minor axis*. The focii will be located along the major axis.

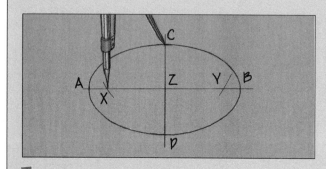

1 **Mark the major axis (AB) and** the minor axis (CD) of the oval on the wood's surface. The axes must be perpendicular to one another and cross at the center (Z). Adjust a compass to half the length of the major axis (AZ or ZB). Put the point of the compass on one end of the minor axis (C or D) and scribe arcs that intersect the major axis (at X and Y). These are the focii of the oval.

2 **Drive two tacks or small** nails at each of the two focii (X and Y). Put a third tack at one end of the major axis (A or B). All three tacks should be in a straight line.

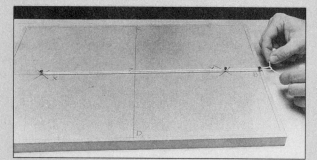

3 **Loop a length of string** around the line of tacks, stretching it tight. Tie the ends together in a square knot.

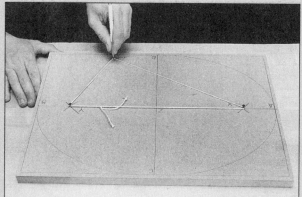

4 **Remove the tack at the end** of the major axis (A or B), but leave the other two tacks and the string in place. Insert the point of a pencil through the square knot and stretch the string taut. Draw the oval, keeping the string taut and pulling it around the tacks.

3

SAWING

Saws are among the oldest woodworking tools. But for much of the four millennia that men and women have been working wood, saws were primitive affairs for roughing out lumber — sturdy blades of bronze or iron with simple round handles. The Romans added some refinements, making the blades thinner, mounting them in frames, and setting the teeth. But it wasn't until the Renaissance that saws became precision tools. Advances in machining and metallurgy made new types of blades available. Within a few hundred years, dozens of saws appeared, from delicate jeweler's saws to fast-cutting carpenter's saws. Today, there seems to be a saw for every type of cut — rip saws for ripping, dovetail saws for dovetails, miter saws for miters, coping saws for coping joints.

Do you need all these handsaws? No. However, most woodworking projects involve some sawing tasks for which it's easier and safer to use a handsaw than a power saw. And there are still a few sawing tasks that can only be accomplished with a handsaw. For both reasons, you should have a small selection of handsaws and know how to use them.

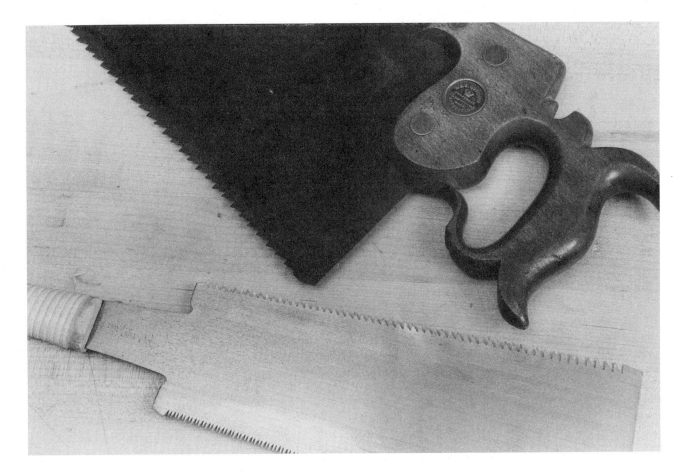

SAW TYPES AND TECHNIQUES

CROSSCUTTING AND RIPPING

While all hand-powered saws are technically *handsaws,* the term usually refers to general-purpose saws for crosscutting and ripping lumber. Handsaws have a thin blade 20 to 30 inches long and a closed handle, sculpted to fit the hand. (*SEE FIGURE 3-1.*) The blade on a good handsaw is *taper ground;* that is, it tapers slightly from the teeth to the back. This helps to keep the saw from binding in a deep cut. The best handles are made from wood — these do not cause the hand to sweat as much as plastic and, if used often enough, will wear to fit the hand of the owner.

Although there were once a dozen or more different types of handsaws, just three are now in common use (*SEE FIGURE 3-2*):

■ A *crosscut* saw cuts across the wood grain. It usually has 8 to 12 teeth per inch, which are sharpened to slice the wood with their edges.

■ A *rip* saw cuts with the wood grain. It has 3 to 7 teeth per inch, sharpened to cut with their points.

■ A *panel* saw, also known as a fast crosscut saw, will make a smoother cut and is often used for cutting plywood panels. It usually has 7 teeth per inch but, depending on the manufacturer, may have as many as 12. The teeth are sharpened like those on a crosscut saw and are sometimes *hardened* — the bottom portion of the blade is tempered so the steel is slightly harder than ordinary saw teeth. This hardening keeps the teeth from wearing quickly when cutting abrasive materials. (Plywood, owing to the glue between the plies, is much more abrasive than wood.)

When using a handsaw, clamp the board to be sawed to a workbench or sawhorses; don't try to steady it with your hand. Hold the saw at a low angle and brace it against the back of your thumb to start

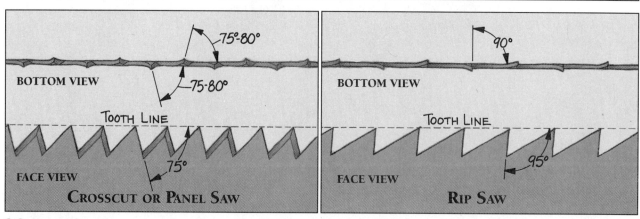

3-1 A handsaw has a thin *blade* (1) and a closed, sculpted *handle* (2). The *teeth* (3) are ground on the bottom of the blade, running all the way from the *toe* (4) to the *heel* (5). The *back* (6) has no teeth.

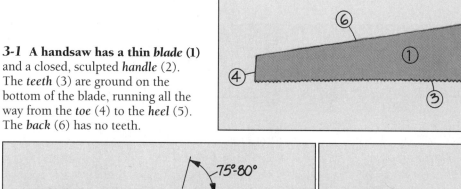

3-2 *Crosscut* teeth are ground and sharpened so the leading edges are about 75 degrees from the tooth line (an imaginary line drawn across the tops of the teeth), and each edge is 75 to 80 degrees from the face of the blade. These teeth slice the wood

grain with their edges. *Rip* teeth, on the other hand, are ground and sharpened so the leading edges are about 95 degrees from the tooth line, and each edge is square to the blade. The points of the teeth are small chisels that cut away the wood.

Note: Crosscut teeth are said to be *sloped* because the leading edges are less than 90 degrees from the tooth line, while rip teeth are *hooked* because their edges are more than 90 degrees.

the cut. (*See Figure 3-3.*) Then change to the best angle for the job — this is determined by the type of saw you're using and the results you want. Use 90 degrees for fast rip cuts, 60 degrees for smooth rips, 45 degrees for rough crosscuts, and 20 degrees for fine crosscuts. (*See Figure 3-4.*)

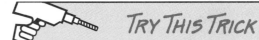

Try This Trick

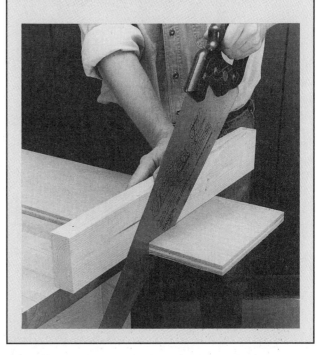

To help keep the cut square, hold a large, square block of wood next to the saw as you work. A two-by-four cutoff works well.

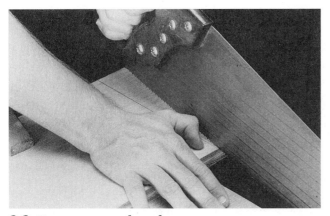

3-3 To start a cut, place the saw so the teeth rest on the *waste* side of the cut line. Hold the blade at a low angle and brace one side of the blade against the back of your thumb, as shown. Make a few light strokes, letting the teeth cut into the wood.

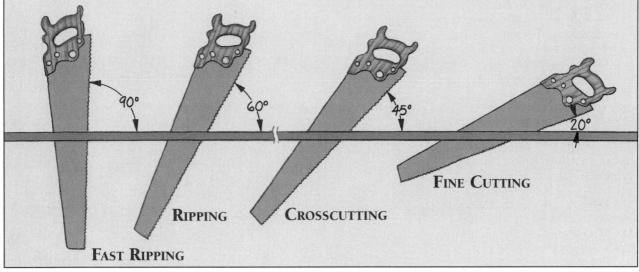

90°   60°   45°   20°

Fast Ripping   **Ripping**   **Crosscutting**   **Fine Cutting**

3-4 Once you've started the cut, hold the blade at the optimum angle for the type of saw you're using and the results you want. To rip a board as quickly as possible, hold the saw nearly perpendicular to the board; for a smoother rip cut, hold it at about a 60-degree angle. For general crosscutting, hold the saw blade 45 degrees from the board; for as fine a crosscut as possible, use a very low angle. Continue to follow the line so the saw cuts on the waste side.

The familiar handsaw design originated in Europe and America, but the Japanese have developed vastly different saws that do the same tasks. These general-purpose saws have gained a large following among western craftsmen in recent years. There are several types that roughly correspond to European/American handsaws (*SEE FIGURE 3-5*):

■ The *ryoba* is the most versatile of the Japanese saws. It's actually two saws in one — the teeth along one edge of the blade are made for crosscutting, while those along the other edge are for ripping. The crosscut edge normally has 14 to 17 teeth per inch, while the rip edge has 7 to 11.

■ The *anahiki* is a fast-cutting saw with *combination* teeth — teeth that are ground to be used for both ripping and crosscutting. There are 5 to 6 teeth per inch and they are larger than on most Japanese saws, so the cut is rougher. However, it's a good general-purpose saw.

■ The *kataba noko* has a stiff blade, 14 to 15 teeth per inch, and the teeth are buttressed so it can be used to cut plywood. (Most Japanese saws aren't recommended for abrasive materials; the teeth are too fragile.)

Although they perform the same tasks, these Japanese saws differ from their European/American counterparts in several significant ways. The blade is shorter and is often wider at the toe than at the heel. The handle is a wooden stick wrapped with a reed to provide a better grip. The gullets between the teeth are much deeper and the teeth are sharpened at steeper angles. (*SEE FIGURE 3-6.*) The biggest difference,

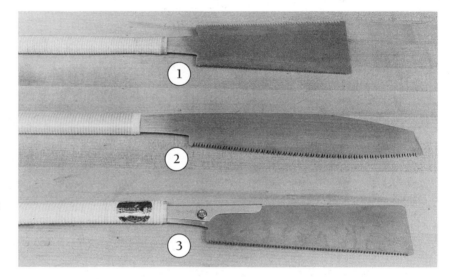

3-5 The *ryoba* (1) is the most versatile (and the most popular) Japanese saw. The blade has two sets of teeth, one for crosscutting and the other for ripping. The *anahiki* (2) is a combination saw for fast, rough cuts, and the *kataba noko* (3) can be used to cut plywood.

3-6 Like their western counter-parts, Japanese *crosscut* teeth cut with their edges. However, the gullets between the teeth are much deeper and they have a secondary angle on the point to help strengthen the long teeth. Japanese *rip* teeth are also similar to those on western rip saws, but their gullets are slightly deeper and they have more of a "hook" — a larger angle between the leading edge and the tooth line. In addition to these design differences, Japanese saw blades are tempered slightly harder than western blades, and this makes them brittle. The teeth stay sharp longer, but they are more fragile.

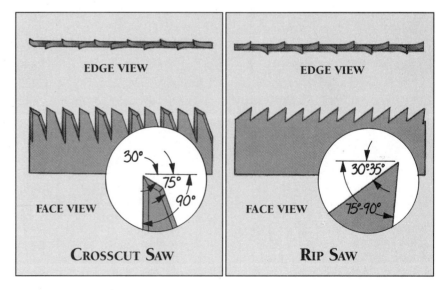

however, is in the way they are used. Japanese saws cut on the *pull* stroke. (European/American saws cut as you *push*.) The saw is under tension as it cuts so the blade can be much thinner. This, in turn, produces a finer cut and a narrower kerf. (*See Figure 3-7.*)

CUTTING JOINERY

While general-purpose saws must be able to make long, deep cuts, joinery saws are intended for short, shallow cutting chores. Additionally, they leave a smoother, flatter surface. There are several types (*see Figure 3-8*):

■ A *tenon saw* (also called a backsaw or rebate saw) is the basic cutting tool for joinery. The thin blade is stiffened with a metal spine to keep it from flexing, and it has 12 to 20 crosscut teeth per inch.

The stiffness and number of teeth allow you to make straight, smooth cuts. (*See Figure 3-9.*)

■ A *dovetail saw* is a smaller version of the tenon saw with a simpler handle, thinner blade, and up to 26 teeth per inch. The teeth may have either a crosscut or a rip grind. It's intended for delicate, exacting cutting tasks, such as sawing the tails and pins in a dovetail joint. (*See Figure 3-10.*) In catalogs, small, short dovetail saws are sometimes referred to as "gent's saws," but this is a misnomer. Originally, a gent's saw was a short crosscut handsaw, and these are no longer commonly available.

■ A *flush-cutting saw* has up to 20 teeth per inch, and these are set to *one side only*. This lets you rest the blade flat on a wood surface and trim protruding wooden parts, such as dowels or wedges. (*See Figure 3-11.*)

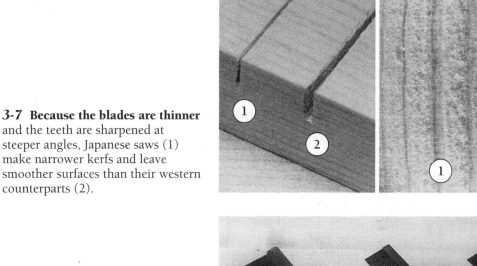

3-7 Because the blades are thinner and the teeth are sharpened at steeper angles, Japanese saws (1) make narrower kerfs and leave smoother surfaces than their western counterparts (2).

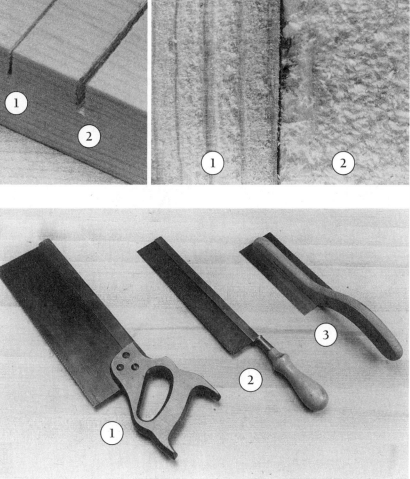

3-8 When cutting wood joinery by hand, a *tenon saw* (1) makes a smooth, straight cut. A *dovetail saw* (2) is necessary for small, exacting work, and a *flush-cutting saw* (3) will trim protruding wooden parts.

3-9 The basic technique for using a tenon saw is to keep it roughly parallel to the surface of the board you're cutting — this produces the smoothest, straightest cut possible. A tenon saw is sometimes used with a hardwood *miter box* (1) to help guide the cut or a shopmade *bench hook* (2) to hold the wood and protect the workbench surface.

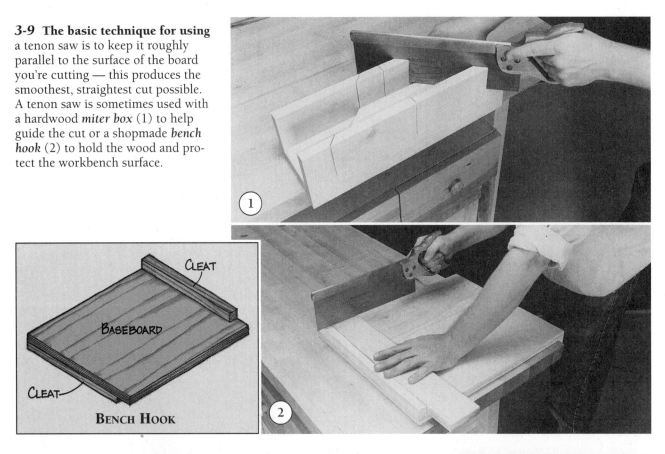

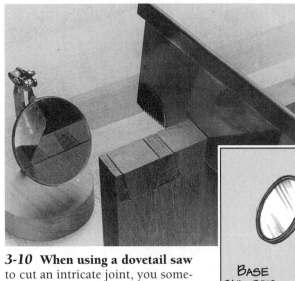

3-10 When using a dovetail saw to cut an intricate joint, you sometimes have to keep an eye on the layout lines on *both* sides of the board. To do this without a lot of head bobbing and neck craning, make this *third eye* jig. Cut off the handle of a small inspection mirror (available at most automotive stores) and mount it in a base.

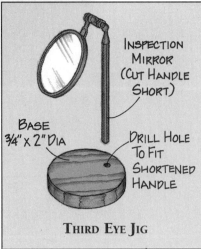

3-11 On a flush-cutting saw, every other tooth is set to *one side only*. The teeth in between aren't set at all. This lets you rest the blade flat on a wood surface, set teeth up, and trim protruding dowels, plugs, wedges, and tenons. Because the teeth are set to just one side and these teeth are facing up, the saw won't scratch the surface.

There are also Japanese versions of these joinery saws. A *dozuki* does the same jobs as a tenon saw or a dovetail saw. A *kugihiki* is used like a flush-cutting saw. (*SEE FIGURE 3-12.*)

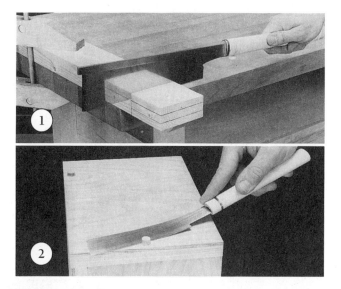

3-12 A Japanese *dozuki* (1) does the same jobs as European/American tenon and dovetail saws. It has a thin blade backed with a metal spine and up to 26 crosscut teeth per inch. A *kugihiki* (2) is used for flush cutting. The blade is extremely flexible, and the teeth have no set at all. Like most Japanese saws, the dozuki and the kugihiki cut on the pull stroke.

TRY THIS TRICK

To cut to a precise depth, fasten a depth stop to a tenon saw or a dovetail saw. The depth stop shown is a wooden shell that fits over the saw blade. Raise or lower the shell to the desired height, then tighten the knobs to fasten it in place.

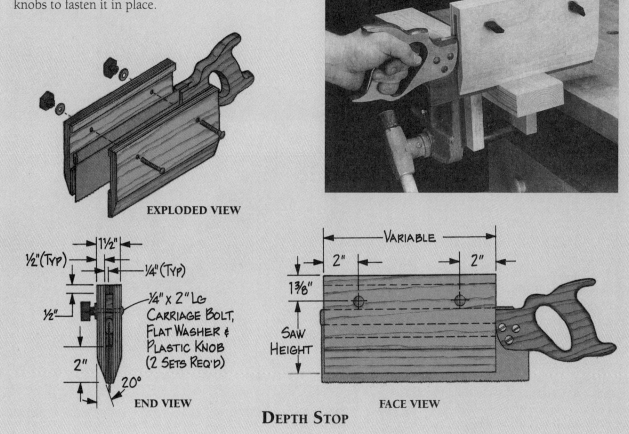

EXPLODED VIEW

¹⁄₂"(TYP)
1¹⁄₂"
¹⁄₄"(TYP)
¹⁄₂"
¹⁄₄" x 2" LG CARRIAGE BOLT, FLAT WASHER & PLASTIC KNOB (2 SETS REQ'D)
2"
20°
END VIEW

VARIABLE
2"   2"
1³⁄₈"
SAW HEIGHT
FACE VIEW

DEPTH STOP

CUTTING CURVES AND CONTOURS

In addition to making straight cuts, woodworkers must also cut curves and contours. Once again, there are several saws designed to do this:

■ A *frame saw* is an ancient tool with contemporary applications. It was developed by the Romans and is still used by European cabinetmakers much like a handsaw. In America, however, it's mostly used to cut gentle curves. The frame can mount many different blades, wide and narrow, with as many or as few teeth per inch as desired. (*See Figure 3-13.*)

■ *Coping saws* and *fret saws* are small metal-frame saws that mount narrow blades. Coping saws have 4- to 5-inch-deep frames and are used for making coped joints and tight curves near the ends or edges of workpieces. Fret saws have a much deeper frame to allow cutting well inside a panel. They also mount a wider variety of blades and are useful for many specialized sawing tasks, such as marquetry, inlay, and scroll work. (*See Figures 3-14 through 3-16.*)

■ A *keyhole saw* (also known as a pad saw or a compass saw) has a stiff, slender blade mounted to a handle. The blade is often taper ground (making it easier to cut curves) and has 8 to 10 teeth per inch. (*See Figure 3-17.*) There is also a Japanese version of the keyhole saw known as a *hikimawashi*.

3-13 A *frame saw* (or bow saw) holds a thin, narrow blade under constant tension, allowing you to cut curves and contours. If you have trouble following the line, the blade may be too loose. Use the toggle stick (1) to twist the tensioning cord (2) a little tighter — this draws in the top ends of the cheeks (the sides of the frame) and pulls out the bottom ends, putting more tension on the blade. When the blade is as tight as you want, let the end of the toggle stick rest against the stretcher (3). This will keep the tensioning cord from unwinding.

3-14 A *coping saw* (1) has a shal- low metal frame that holds *pin-end* (2) blades. A *fret saw* (3) has a much deeper frame and holds *plain-end* (4) blades. Pin-end blades are easier to mount, but there is a much wider variety of plain-end blades. Consequently, coping saws are used for general curve cutting close to the edge of a workpiece, while fret saws cut deep inside a board and can be used for many specialized tasks.

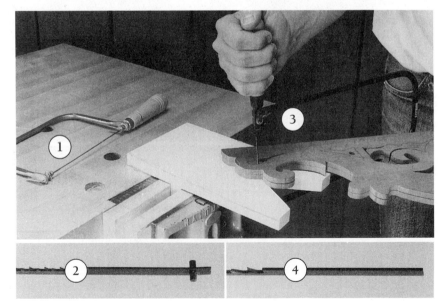

3-15 This fret-sawing table
mounts in a vise and supports a
workpiece when cutting with either
a fret saw or a coping saw. Mount a
blade in the frame so the teeth point
down — this will hold the wood on
the table. As you cut, gently press the
blade into the V-shaped cutout. This
keeps the wood and the blade from
sliding around and gives you better
control.

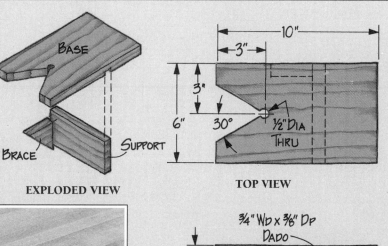

EXPLODED VIEW

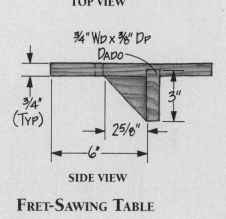

TOP VIEW

SIDE VIEW

FRET-SAWING TABLE

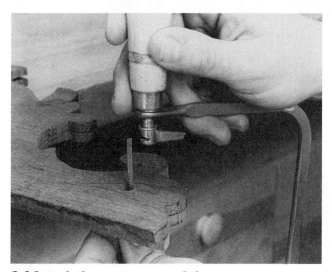

3-16 Both the coping saw and the
fret saw can be used to make *interior*
cuts — sawing inside the perimeter
of a board without cutting through
from the ends or edges. Lay out the
pattern on the workpiece and drill a
hole through the waste where you
want to make an interior cut. Insert
the blade through the hole, mount it
in the saw frame, and begin cutting.

3-17 A *keyhole saw* will also make
curves and interior cuts. It doesn't
cut as smoothly or turn as sharp a
radius as a coping saw or a fret saw,
but it can be used in places where it
would be awkward or impossible to
use these frame-mounted saws.

SAWS FOR OTHER MATERIALS

Most woodworkers must also do a little metalworking. Occasionally, you need to cut off a bolt or a screw, maintain or fix a tool, or modify a piece of hardware. For this, you need a *hacksaw*. Like a coping saw, a hacksaw mounts a blade in a metal frame. The blades, however, are made from high-quality tool steel and tempered so they are harder than most of the metal objects in your shop. (*See Figure 3-18.*)

Hacksaw blades may have anywhere from 8 to 32 teeth per inch. The thinner the metal you're cutting, the more teeth the blade should have. The teeth are arranged in a "wavy" set so each tooth takes a small bite. (*See Figure 3-19.*)

A BIT OF ADVICE

Don't use a hacksaw to cut wood. The gullets between the teeth are too small to clear the wood chips efficiently. The blade quickly overheats and breaks.

To make curved and contoured cuts in soft metals, bone, mother-of-pearl, plastic, and similar materials, use a *jeweler's saw*. This is similar to a small fret saw, but it mounts jeweler's blades — tiny blades designed to make intricate cuts in thin stock. (*See Figure 3-20.*)

3-18 Coax a hacksaw through metal, don't force it. Use light pressure and slow, steady strokes (about one per second). If you saw quickly or use too much pressure, the blade will heat up and the teeth will dull.

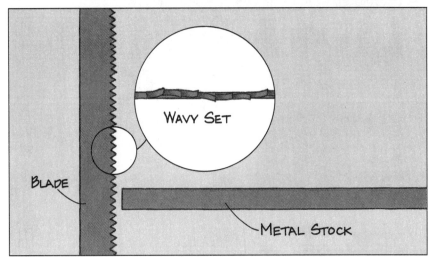

3-19 Hacksaw teeth are arranged in a *wavy* set, as shown. Because each tooth is set just a little farther to one side of the tooth preceding it, the blade takes only a small bite. This keeps the teeth from wearing prematurely when cutting through hard materials. When choosing a hacksaw blade, make sure that it has enough teeth per inch so at least *two* (preferably three) teeth are engaged in the cut at all times; otherwise, the blade will bind. Consequently, the thinner the material, the more teeth per inch the blade should have.

WAVY SET

BLADE

METAL STOCK

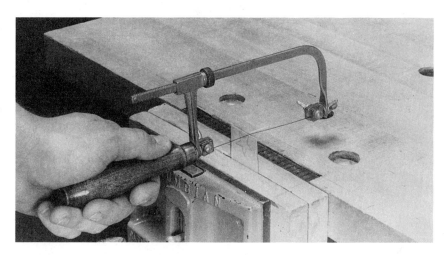

3-20 Make intricate cuts in thin materials with a *jeweler's saw*. The small metal frame holds tiny plain-end blades, from .012 to .024 inch wide. (The blades are numbered from 8/0 to 0 in the "Universal" system used to label scroll and fret blades.) Although these blades will not cut hard steel, they are hard enough for mild steel, soft metal, bone, and plastic. They may also be used to cut veneer, posterboard, and even paper, although they break more frequently when cutting softer materials.

CARING FOR SAWS

STORAGE

To keep your saws sharp, *protect the teeth* just as you would protect the newly sharpened edge of a chisel or knife blade. Be careful where and how you lay the saw down — hardened glue beads, sanding grit, and other metal tools can nick or break a tooth. When you aren't using the saw, hang it up or put it away in a cabinet or a tool chest. If possible, cover the teeth. (*SEE FIGURE 3-21.*)

SHARPENING

It's usually worth your while to take your handsaws to a professional sharpener when they're dull. You cannot achieve the same precision with hand files and guides that a pro can with a sharpening machine. Still, there are times when it's handy to be able to sharpen your own saws — after all, the sharpening shop isn't open every day of the week.

To sharpen a handsaw, you'll need a mill file, a saw jointer, a saw set, and a triangular file. Begin by cleaning the saw and inspecting the teeth for damage. Compare the unused teeth near the heel of the blade with those toward the middle. Are the used teeth worn? Are any teeth broken? This will give you a good idea of how much work you have to do.

If the teeth are extremely worn or damaged, *joint* them flat and even with a mill file — that is, file them to the same height. (*SEE FIGURE 3-22.*) When you joint, you must file down the tops of the unused teeth more than those that are already worn down. If you remove more than one-third of the height of any one tooth, you'll have to recut or *shape* the teeth with a triangular file. (*SEE FIGURES 3-23 AND 3-24.*) When it's necessary to shape the teeth, you must also *set* them, alternately bending them to the left and right. (*SEE FIGURE 3-25.*) Finally, *sharpen* the teeth with a fine (smooth-cut) triangular file. File rip saws straight across and crosscut saws at an angle of 75 to 80 degrees. (*SEE FIGURE 3-26.*)

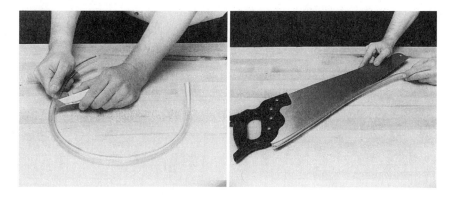

3-21 To protect your saws and keep them sharp, cover the teeth when you aren't using them. Many saws come with snap-on or strap-on protectors. Or, you can make your own protector from a length of vinyl tubing. Split the tubing lengthwise with a utility knife, then insert the saw teeth into the split.

FOR BEST RESULTS

Many new handsaws are not sharpened by the manufacturer; the teeth are simply stamped and set. They cut reasonably well at first because the stamping leaves sharp burrs on the teeth, but the burrs dull quickly. A new saw will cut a whole lot better if you take the time to sharpen it — or have it sharpened — before you use it.

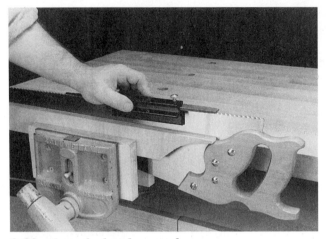

3-22 Clean the handsaw and inspect the teeth. If the used teeth in the middle of the saw are worn down more than the teeth at the heel, or if the teeth have been damaged, joint the teeth with a mill file. Clamp the file in a saw jointer and run it along the teeth until they are all the same height. You know they're all at the same height when there's a small, shiny spot on the tops of all the teeth.

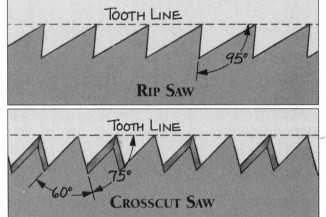

3-23 When jointing removes more than one-third of the height of any of the teeth, you must also recut the tooth shapes with a triangular file. Clamp the saw between two long scraps of plywood to hold it rigid. If you're sharpening a rip saw, hold the file so it will cut hooked teeth with faces about 95 degrees from the tooth line. For a crosscut saw, hold the file to cut sloped teeth with faces about 75 degrees from the tooth line.

3-24 To cut all the gullets between the teeth to the same depth, align the plywood scraps so they are about 1/16 inch below the old gullets (before filing) and parallel to the tooth line. File the gullets until the file reaches the plywood. Inspect the teeth; they should all be pointed, with no shiny flat spots on the tips. If any flat spots remain, readjust the plywood scraps and file the gullets another 1/32 inch deeper. Repeat until the flat spots disappear and the teeth are all properly shaped.

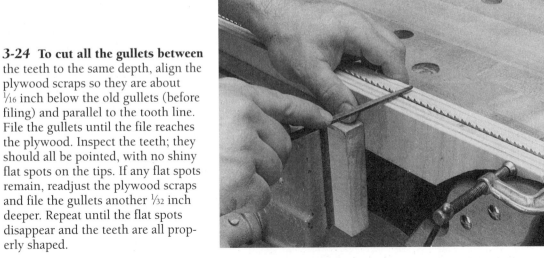

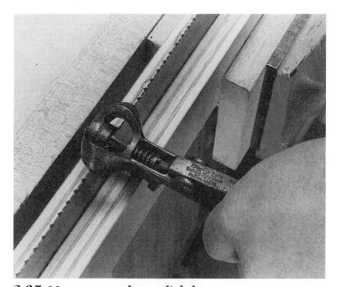

3-25 Most saw teeth are slightly bent or *set* right or left so they will cut a kerf that's slightly wider than the body of the saw. (The rule of thumb is to make the set one-third the thickness of the saw blade.) This prevents the saw from binding in the cut. After jointing and shaping, bend the teeth with a saw set, a hand tool especially made for this purpose. Adjust the tool for the proper set (the distance it bends each tooth), then bend every other tooth to the right. Go back and bend the teeth in between to the left. **Note:** Although you can buy new saw sets through mail-order woodworking suppliers, you can often find a used set for a few dollars at a flea market or a garage sale.

3-26 Using a triangular file, sharpen the edges of the teeth. To sharpen a rip saw, file straight across the teeth, perpendicular to the saw blade. For a crosscut saw, first file the teeth that are set to the right, working from the left side of the saw. Switch sides and file the teeth that are set to the left. Hold the file 75 to 80 degrees from the saw blade, and use a shopmade guide block to help maintain the angle and keep it consistent from tooth to tooth.

RUST PREVENTION AND LUBRICATION

To prevent saw blades from rusting, apply a coat of paste wax to the metal surfaces and buff it out — this seals the metal from moisture. If you store your saws for long periods of time between uses, wax them *before* you put them away. **Note:** Be sure to buff out the wax after you apply it. This reduces the wax to a thin coat no more than a few molecules thick. If you leave a thick application on the blade, it will rub off on the wood and interfere with the finish.

The paste wax also cleans and lubricates the saw blade, reducing friction and helping it glide through the wood. Some craftsmen keep a block of paraffin in their tool kits to rub on saw blades for just this purpose. This works well, especially for rough cuts with handsaws. However, paraffin may create the same problem as excess paste wax — it will rub off on the wood and interfere with a finish. Waxing and buffing is a better all-around solution.

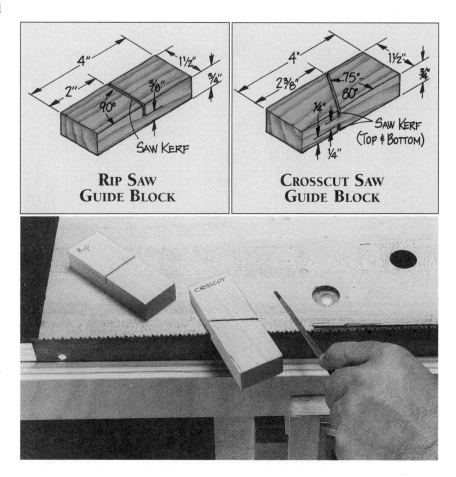

4

SURFACING AND SHAPING

The invention of the hand plane is usually credited to the ancient Greeks, although there is some evidence that the Greeks borrowed the idea from craftsmen in Asia Minor. The origin of the scraper is even less certain; it appears to be an even older device. Whomever we have to thank, both tools represent quantum leaps in woodworking. The hand plane enabled craftsmen to shave a wooden surface with an ease and precision that was otherwise impossible; the scraper left the surface satin smooth. Since their introduction, planes and scrapers have been devised for smoothing boards, cutting joinery, creating shapes, and many other tasks. By the early nineteenth century, a well-equipped cabinet shop often had over 100 planing and scraping tools, each with a specific purpose.

Nowadays, much of this work is done with machines such as planers, jointers, shapers, and routers. But hand planes and scrapers remain the hallmark of fine woodworking. For many exacting woodworking tasks, there is often no better tool than a plane. And nothing can get a wood surface smoother quicker than a scraper. For these reasons, most experienced craftsmen still use a modest selection of planes and scrapers.

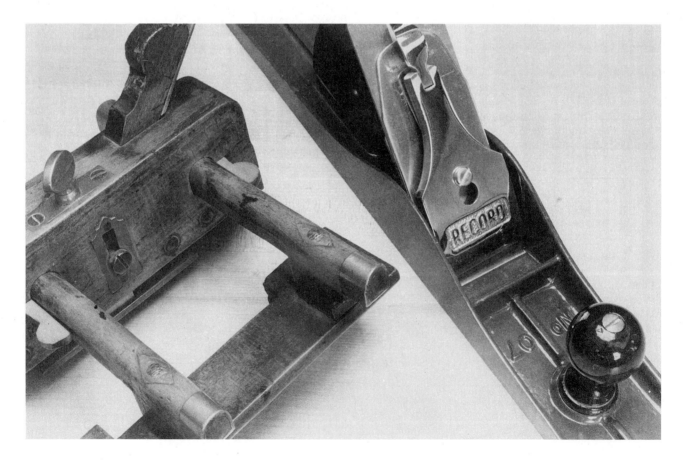

SMOOTHING AND TRIMMING

PLANE ANATOMY

For over 2,000 years, planes were simple affairs — steel blades in wooden cradles, held in place with wedges. Most were handmade by the craftsmen who used them. In the early nineteenth century, tool manufacturers began to offer ready-made planes with improved features — metal parts, better blade support, and devices for adjusting the depth of cut.

Today, the most commonly used plane — the *bench plane* — has a metal *body* with a long, flat *sole* and two wooden *handles*. The blade or *plane iron* is mounted on an adjustable *frog*, a mechanism that not only supports the blade but allows you to adjust its position both front to back and side to side. The plane iron is covered with a cap iron or *chip breaker* to break up the shavings and keep them from clogging the tool. The plane iron and chip breaker are held to the frog by a *lever cap*. (SEE FIGURE 4-1.) The frog, chip breaker, and lever cap reinforce the plane iron and make it extremely rigid. This, in turn, helps the plane cut smoother and with less effort.

SURFACING PLANES

Bench planes are just one type of surfacing plane. You can also use block planes and palm planes for surfacing operations. (SEE FIGURE 4-2.)

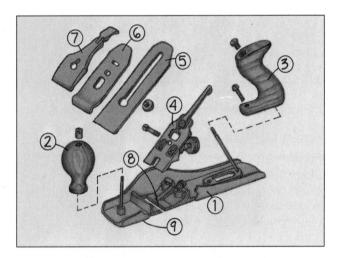

4-1 There are many types of hand planes, but the most common is the **bench plane**. The **body** (1) of this plane supports a **front handle** (2), a **rear handle** (3), and an adjustable **frog** (4). The frog holds the **plane iron** (5) and allows you to adjust its position. The iron is covered with a **chip breaker** (6), and a **lever cap** (7) holds the iron and the chip breaker to the frog. The cutting edge of the iron extends down through the **mouth** (8), a narrow opening in the bottom or **sole** (9) of the plane.

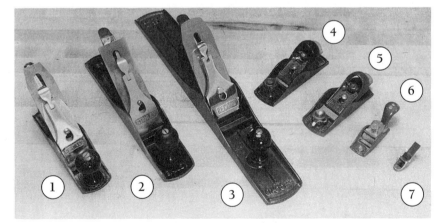

4-2 There are three types of hand planes for general surfacing — bench planes, block planes, and palm planes. Bench planes are distinguished by their length. A short bench plane, less than 11 inches long, is called a **smooth plane** (1) and is used for smoothing a surface. A **jack plane** (2), between 14 and 15 inches long, is an all-purpose plane. A **jointer** or **try plane** (3) is over 18 inches long and is used for truing surfaces and edges of boards. Block planes are characterized by their cutting angle — a **standard block plane** (4) has the same cutting angle (45 degrees) as most planes, while the cutting angle of a **low-angle block plane** (5) is 8 degrees lower. A **palm plane** (6) is defined by its size. Some fit in the palm of your hand; others, known as **finger planes** (7), are so small they must be held between two fingers.

Bench planes have long, flat soles, and the plane iron is mounted with the bevel *down*. The length of the sole determines the plane's purpose. *Smooth planes,* with soles less than 11 inches, are used for smoothing stock. *Try planes,* with soles over 18 inches long, will flatten surfaces and joint edges. *Jack planes,* which are in between, are used for general-purpose planing. **Note:** The longer the bench plane, the wider the plane iron. Smooth plane irons are commonly 1¾ inches wide; jack planes, 2 inches wide; and try planes, 2⅜ inches wide.

Block planes are smaller and shorter than bench planes, and the irons are mounted with the bevel *up*. There is no frog or chip breaker; the iron is held directly to the body with a lever cap. Most block planes have an adjustable mouth. By changing the size of this opening, you can control chatter and tear-out. The prevailing opinion is that block planes are best for shaving end grain, but this isn't necessarily so. The cutting angles of a *standard* block plane and a bench plane are the same, so neither has an advantage over the other when cutting end grain. (*See Figure 4-3.*)

Only a *low-angle* block plane has a slight advantage; its cutting angle is 8 degrees lower than either a bench plane or a standard block plane. The real benefit of a block plane is its size — this tool is designed to be used with one hand and is ideal for small surfacing and trimming jobs.

Palm planes are even smaller and simpler in construction than block planes. The plane iron, which is mounted with the bevel *down*, as in a bench plane, is held directly to the body with a wedge or a screw cap. There is no apparatus for positioning the iron, so you must tap the iron with a mallet. If there is a handle, it's usually part of the body. Because of their small size, palm planes will reach places that larger planes won't.

When purchasing bench, block, and palm planes, there are several options to consider:

■ Should the plane body be *wood* or *metal*? Metal wears better, but many woodworkers prefer the look and feel of wood. (*See Figure 4-4.*)

■ If you choose a metal plane, should the sole be *flat* or *ribbed* (also known as corrugated)? Ribbing reduces the area of the sole that contacts the wood, and this reduces the friction and makes the plane easier to push across the surface. (*See Figure 4-5.*)

■ Do you prefer *European* or *Japanese* planes? European planes are generally pushed across the wood surface; Japanese planes are pulled.

■ Do you require an *adjusting screw* or a *screw-and-lever* mechanism to set the iron angle and depth of cut? If the plane iron is simply wedged in the body, you must learn to adjust the iron by tapping on it. (*See Figure 4-6.*) This takes more time and finesse than just turning a screw.

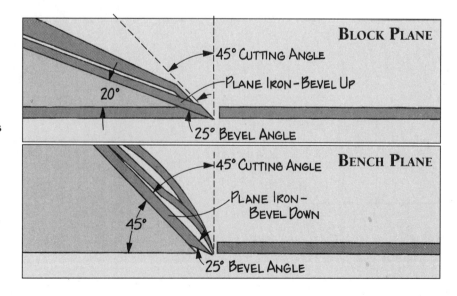

4-3 A standard block plane holds its plane iron at 20 degrees, while a bench plane holds it at 45 degrees. You might think that a block plane would slice the wood at a lower angle, but this isn't so. Because the iron is mounted bevel up in a block plane and bevel down in a bench plane, the cutting angles are the same. Both planes are designed for general planing chores.

With the possible exception of the adjusting mechanism, few of these features are critical to the function of a surfacing plane. Remember that in most woodworking shops, planes may still be necessary but they are no longer used constantly. Even though metal wears longer than wood, it's unlikely that you will wear out a wooden plane in your lifetime. And although a ribbed plane requires less muscle power, it's equally unlikely that you wear yourself out pushing a plane with a solid sole across your work. Use whatever plane appeals to you — that's the one that will probably work best for you.

4-4 Although most modern planes have metal bodies (left), there are still a few that are made from wood (right). Metal planes were the first to be made with an adjustment mechanism for the plane iron, and this enticed nineteenth-century woodworkers to abandon their old wooden planes in favor of the latest cast-iron models. Today, both types of commercially made planes have adjusting mechanisms, and both are excellent tools. Realistically, metal planes still offer a slight advantage because they wear longer and are less expensive than the wooden planes available today. However, you risk starting a holy war if you say that in a room full of woodworkers — many craftsmen believe in one type or the other with the fervor of religious fanatics.

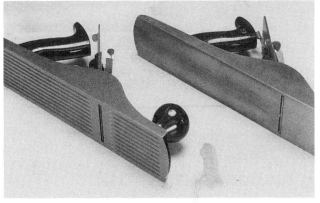

4-5 Some large bench planes have *ribbed* soles rather then flat ones. Ribbing reduces the weight of the plane and the friction between the wood and the metal. This, in turn, makes the plane easier to push without interfering with the cutting action. Ribbed planes are, however, considerably more expensive than ones with flat soles. If you need a plane for occasional surfacing chores, the ribbing is not worth the expense.

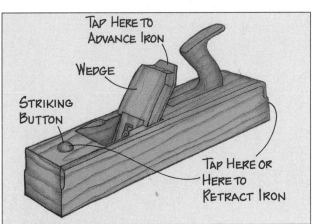

4-6 If the plane iron is secured in the plane with a simple wedge, you must adjust the depth of cut with a small mallet. To advance the iron for a deeper cut, tap its back edge *very lightly*. To retract the blade, tap one end of the plane body. Some planes have **striking buttons** near the toe or the heel just for this purpose. Once the iron is set, tap the back of the wedge one or two times to seat it.

USING A HAND PLANE

Before using a hand plane to cut anything important, make sure the blade is sharp and properly adjusted. If the plane has a chip breaker, set it 1/16 to 1/8 inch away from the cutting edge for rough work, or 1/32 to 1/16 inch away for fine work.

Secure the iron in the plane with the cutting edge parallel to the mouth opening but not protruding from the mouth. While passing the plane across a clear wood scrap, *slowly* advance the iron either by turning the adjusting screw or by tapping the end of the iron. When the iron begins to take a shaving, check that it's cutting all across the width of the cutting edge. (*See Figure 4-7.*) If not, readjust the angle of the iron, either by moving a lever from side to side or by tapping on the sides of the iron. When the plane is cutting a paper-thin shaving as wide as the iron, it's ready to use.

When making the initial *roughing cuts* on a board to true the surface, pass the plane across the wood at a steep diagonal to the wood grain. When making *smoothing cuts* to smooth the surface, hold the plane at a slight angle to the wood grain but push (or pull) the plane parallel to it. (*See Figure 4-8.*) To keep from dulling the plane iron prematurely, don't drag the plane backward across the wood when you finish a pass. Lift it up to return it for the next pass.

4-7 It's just as important to adjust the angle of a plane iron as it is the depth of cut. You know the depth of cut is correct when the plane is cutting a paper-thin shaving. The angle is correct when the plane is cutting a shaving as wide as the plane iron.

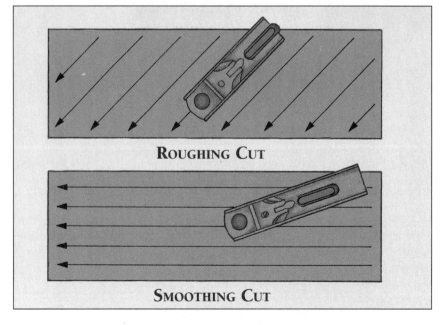

ROUGHING CUT

SMOOTHING CUT

4-8 To remove stock from a board quickly, push the plane over the surface at a steep diagonal to the wood grain. This is called a *roughing cut,* and, as the name implies, it does not leave a particularly smooth surface. When a smooth surface is desired, make a *smoothing cut* — hold the plane at a slight diagonal to the wood grain and pass it across the surface parallel to the grain.

FOR YOUR INFORMATION

It's easier to push the plane, and you get a finer cut, when you hold the plane at an angle to its direction of travel. This is because the cutting angle increases, as shown in the drawings. In effect, the plane iron is shaving the wood from a lower angle.

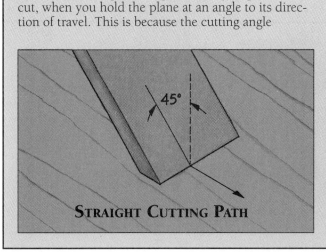

STRAIGHT CUTTING PATH

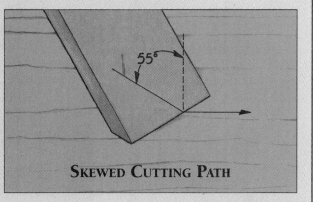

SKEWED CUTTING PATH

With a sharp, properly adjusted bench plane, you can prepare rough-cut lumber as well as you might with a jointer and a planer. You may not have to do this very often, but it's good to know, especially if you reproduce classic designs or want to achieve the gently undulating surfaces associated with old heirloom pieces. To prepare lumber with a hand plane, first flatten one face of the board. (*SEE FIGURE 4-9.*) Score the ends and edges, marking the thickness all around the board's perimeter, then plane the second face parallel to the first. (*SEE FIGURE 4-10.*) Plane one edge straight, cut the board the width, and plane the second edge parallel to the first. (*SEE FIGURE 4-11.*) Finally, cut the board to length. If necessary, square up the ends with a plane and a *shooting board.* (*SEE FIGURE 4-12.*)

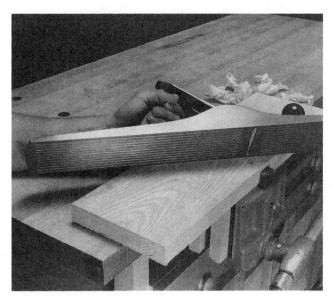

4-9 To prepare rough-cut lumber for use with a hand plane, first true one face of the board, planing it as flat as possible. Use the edge of the plane as a straightedge to check your work.

4-10 When one face is flat, scribe the thickness of the board all around the perimeter, on both ends and edges. (Make certain that the marking gauge stop bears against the trued face as you do this.) Plane the second face parallel to the first, stopping when you reach the scribed lines.

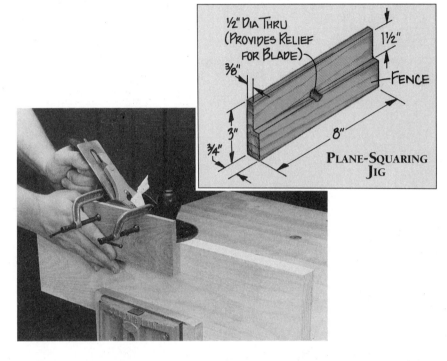

PLANE-SQUARING JIG

4-11 After truing the faces, true the edges. Plane the first edge straight and square. Then cut the board to within ¹⁄₁₆ inch of the desired width. Plane the second edge straight, square, and parallel to the first. To help keep the plane's sole square to the face of the board when planing long stock, make this simple jig and clamp it to the plane body. Hold the fence firmly against the board as you work.

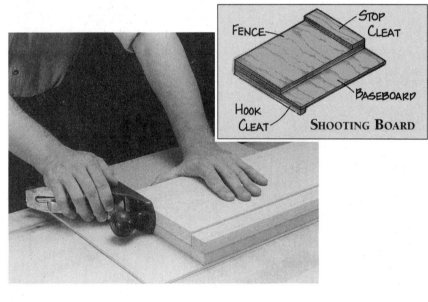

SHOOTING BOARD

4-12 When the board is planed to the proper thickness and width, cut it to length. If you wish, plane the ends of the board perfectly square with the aid of a *shooting board.* Lay the plane on its side so the cutting edge of the plane iron is vertical. Guide the sole along the fence, holding the wood against the plane and the stop at the back of the jig. **Note:** You can also use a shooting board to plane the edge of short stock.

TRIMMING PLANES

Although most planes are intended for general surfacing, there are some special-purpose planes designed for specific trimming operations. Most of these are made to trim joints in one way or another and are used primarily when fitting pieces of wood together.

Rabbet planes, for example, are designed to trim the surfaces in rabbets, tenons, lap joints, or any inside corner. The mouth of a rabbet plane is open on both sides of the plane body, and the iron is as wide as or slightly wider than the plane body. This enables a rabbet plane to reach into a corner as you cut *along* it, trimming one surface without disturbing the other. The plane iron is bedded with the bevel up (like a block plane) so the iron can be supported almost to the tip of the cutting edge. This extra support prevents chattering and gives you a smoother cut.

There are four types of rabbet planes (*SEE FIGURE 4-13*):

■ A *fillister plane* is fitted with a removable fence to help guide the plane and make the cut parallel to the edge.

■ A *shoulder plane* (also called a trimming plane) is machined so the sides are perfectly square to the sole. If you hold the side of the plane firmly against one surface of a rabbet, you can cut the other surface square to it. (*SEE FIGURE 4-14.*)

■ A *bullnose plane* is similar to a shoulder plane, but the iron is bedded so the cutting edge is within a fraction of an inch from the toe (front edge) of the sole. This lets you cut much closer to a corner or a stop when you must cut *toward* it.

■ A *chisel plane* (also known as a stop rabbet plane or an edge plane), has the iron mounted on the toe, letting you trim right up to a corner or a stop when cutting toward it. (*SEE FIGURE 4-15.*)

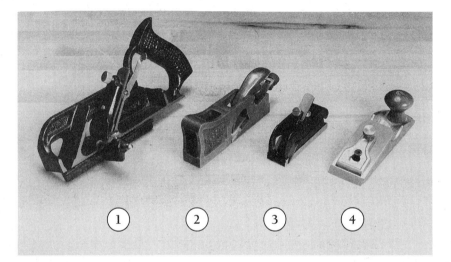

4-13 Rabbet planes are designed to trim the surfaces of inside corners. There are four types: A *fillister plane* (1), a *shoulder plane* (2), a *bullnose plane* (3), and a *chisel plane* (4).

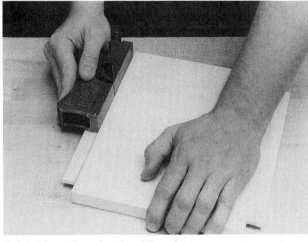

4-14 The sides of a shoulder plane are machined 90 degrees to the sole, making it an indispensable tool for cleaning up and fitting joinery. For example, if you need to trim the shoulder of a tenon, simply rest the side of the plane on the cheek. As long as the plane iron is properly adjusted, the cut will be perfectly square.

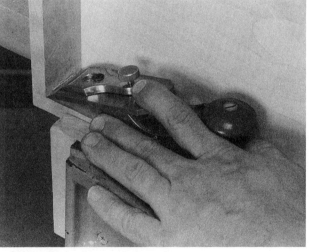

4-15 For those operations where you must cut up to a corner rather than along one, use a chisel plane. Take very light cuts to help keep the wood from splitting. Because this plane has no mouth, it tends to lift the wood ahead of the cutting edge if you make deep cuts.

There are also planes for trimming one surface of an outside corner. An *edge-trimming plane* has a rabbeted sole that wraps around the arris of a board to cut an edge or an end. (*See Figure 4-16.*) A *side-rabbet plane* is designed to cut the sides of a dado or groove. (*See Figure 4-17.*) On both planes, the sole forms an inside corner (two surfaces joined at 90 degrees) and the plane iron is mounted on just one surface.

Finally, a *router plane* will trim the bottom of a dado, groove, or mortise. On this plane, the L-shaped cutting iron protrudes below the sole to reach into recesses. (*See Figure 4-18.*)

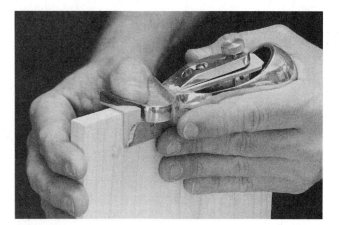

4-16 The sole of an *edge-trimming plane* wraps around an outside corner to trim one surface square to the other. The iron is mounted bevel up, and the cutting edge is usually skewed — this helps reduce the force it takes to cut, especially when planing end grain. This tool is useful when you need to trim a little stock from the edge or end of a board.

TRY THIS TRICK

You can temporarily convert a bevel-edge chisel or a paring chisel to a chisel plane with this simple jig. Just rest the chisel on the bed and tighten the wing nuts to clamp it in place. Adjust the depth of cut by loosening the nuts slightly and sliding the jig up or down the length of the chisel.

¼" x 1" DIA FENDER WASHER

³⁄₁₆" DIA x ³⁄₁₆" DP C'BORE

³⁄₁₆" FLAT WASHER

¼" x 1½" HEX BOLTS & WING NUTS (2 SETS REQ'D)

EXPLODED VIEW

CHISEL PLANE JIG
(HOLDS A ¾", 1", OR 1¼" BEVEL-EDGE CHISEL)

NOTE: Make two chisel holders that are mirror images of each other.

¼" DIA THRU (TYP)

½"

20°

1½" 1¾"

1⁵⁄₁₆"

¾"

4"

SIDE VIEW

³⁄₈"

14°

¼"

ROUT ANGLE WITH DOVETAIL BIT

¾"

END VIEW

CHISEL HOLDER

4-17 A *side-rabbet plane* will trim the sides of a dado or a groove. An adjustable stop controls how far the iron reaches into the recess. Some of these planes have two irons to cut in both directions. The irons are mounted bevel up, and the cutting edges are skewed. These are extremely handy tools when you need to widen a joint by a small amount.

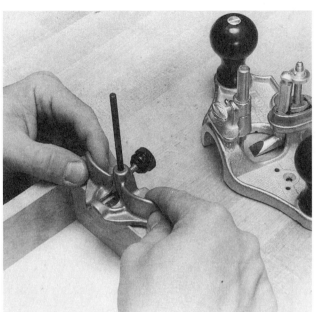

4-18 A *router plane* trims the bottom of a dado, groove, or mortise. Use it to deepen these recesses, cut the bottoms parallel to the wood surface, or cut them to a uniform depth. (The router plane shown is being used to even up the bottom of a hinge mortise.) The L-shaped plane iron protrudes below the sole and you adjust the depth of cut by raising or lowering the iron. Because the cutting edge is unsupported, you'll get better results if you take very shallow cuts.

SHAVES AND DRAWKNIVES

Spokeshaves are special planes designed to cut narrow and rounded stock such as chair rungs or table legs. The body of a spokeshave has two long handles that protrude from each side so you can push or pull it along the stock. It takes a knack to use one of these — you must hold it at the proper angle, slightly skewed to the direction in which you cut. But once you get a little experience, you'll find a spokeshave useful for easing corners, trimming round tenons, and sculpting legs and turnings. (*See Figure 4-19.*)

Drawknives are used in much the same way as spokeshaves — you pull them toward you along the surface of the wood. However, they have no sole to limit the depth of cut, making them more difficult to control. Use the handles to adjust the angle of the blade as you draw it toward you. With a little practice, you can find an angle that will remove a thin, even layer of wood. (*See Figure 4-20.*)

SCRAPING TOOLS

Although hand planes leave a smooth surface, the best tools for smoothing the wood before applying a finish are *scrapers*. As the name implies, these scrape the wood smooth. A scraper has a thin metal blade with a long, sharp *burr* on its edge. The burr shaves the wood, then the blade plows up the cut fibers, removing a thinner-than-paper shaving from the surface. (*See Figure 4-21.*)

There are five types of scraping tools:

■ *Hand scrapers* are thin pieces of tool steel with burred edges that come in various sizes, shapes, and thicknesses. (*See Figure 4-22.*)

■ A *cabinet scraper* mounts the blade in a rigid holder with handles on the sides. You cannot alter the angle of the blade to the work. (*See Figure 4-23.*)

■ A *scraper plane* mounts a blade in an adjustable holder, allowing you to change the blade angle. The holder is similar to a small bench plane.

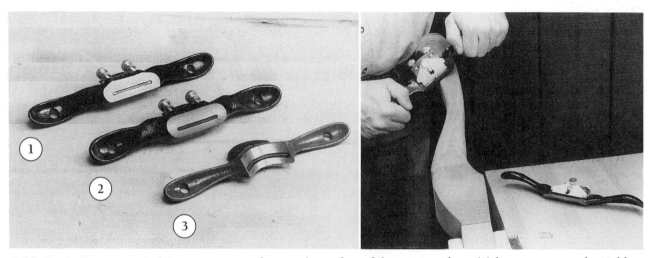

4-19 Spokeshaves are made to plane narrow or round stock. The body has two handles protruding from the sides, and the sole is shaped to conform to the surface of the wood. A *flat spokeshave* (1) has a flat sole, a *round spokeshave* (2) has a convex sole, and a *crescent spoke-* *shave* (3) has a concave sole. Unlike most planes, which are pushed along the wood, spokeshaves can be either pushed or pulled.

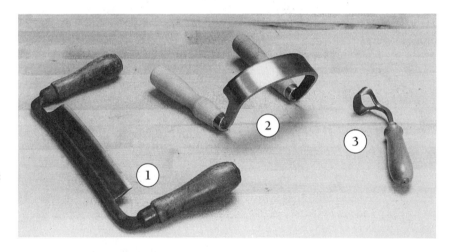

4-20 Drawknives are used much like spokeshaves, and like spokeshaves, there are different shapes to conform to the surface of the wood. A *straight drawknife* (1) has a straight cutting edge; an *inshave* (2) has a curved edge; and the edge of a *scorp* (3) forms a loop. Straight drawknives are not often used in fine woodworking, but inshaves and scorps are employed by chairmakers and carvers to scoop out chair seats, bowls, and recesses.

4-21 Scraping tools all have a thin metal blade with a *burr* on the edge. The burr is usually turned 75 to 80 degrees from the face of the blade. When you hold the blade at a 65- to 70-degree angle to the wood, the burr shaves the surface. As the blade is pushed forward, it acts like a chip breaker, turning the shaving and plowing it up. The rounded, burnished edge just behind the burr serves the same purpose as a pressure bar on a planer and helps prevent the wood fibers from tearing. This lets you scrape a smooth surface on all sorts of wood grain and in any direction — it doesn't matter whether you scrape straight or figured grain.

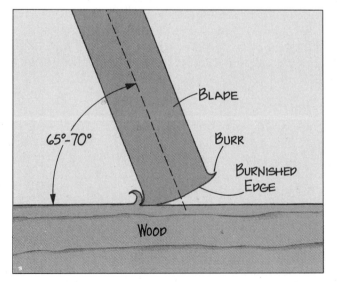

■ *Shavehooks* have a handle to pull the blade along the wood. The blade comes in several shapes and sizes. (*SEE FIGURE 4-24.*)

■ *Molding scrapers* are similar to shavehooks, but they are smaller and the blades are more intricately shaped.

The technique for using all these scraping tools is similar. Adjust or hold the blade at a slight angle to the surface, then push or pull it so the burr shaves the wood. Don't drag the tool back across the wood on the return stroke; this will dull the burr. Pick it up off the surface before returning it for another pass.

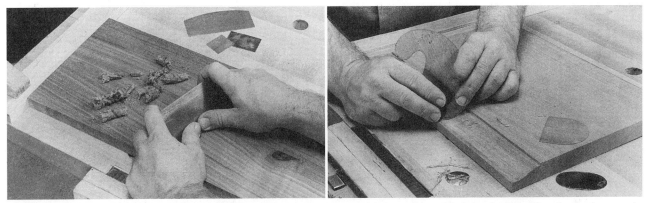

4-22 To use a *hand scraper*, hold the blade slightly off vertical, angled 15 to 20 degrees in the direction of the cut. Push or pull the blade along the wood surface, pressing down and varying the angle as you do so. When you feel the burr bite into the wood, hold that angle and continue to move the scraper forward. Choose a blade that conforms to the surface you wish to scrape — straight for flat surfaces, curved for contoured surfaces. Many craftsmen prefer to hold the scraper in two hands, flexing the blade with their thumbs as they push it forward. However, this isn't the only possible technique. You can scrape two-handed or one-handed, flexing or not flexing, pushing or pulling, whatever works best for the task at hand.

4-23 When scraping large, flat areas, a *cabinet scraper* and a *scraping plane* are somewhat easier to use than a hand scraper, which can be tiresome to hold and flex. These tools hold the blade at the proper angle for you; all there is to do is push.

4-24 *Shavehooks* and *molding* *scrapers* are made to scrape hard-to-reach areas such as corners and shaped surfaces. To use either tool, grasp the handle, push the blade down on the stock, and pull it toward you. Adjust the angle of the blade by raising or lowering the handle. Shavehooks usually come in three shapes — triangular, square, and teardrop. Molding scrapers are available in a much wider variety.

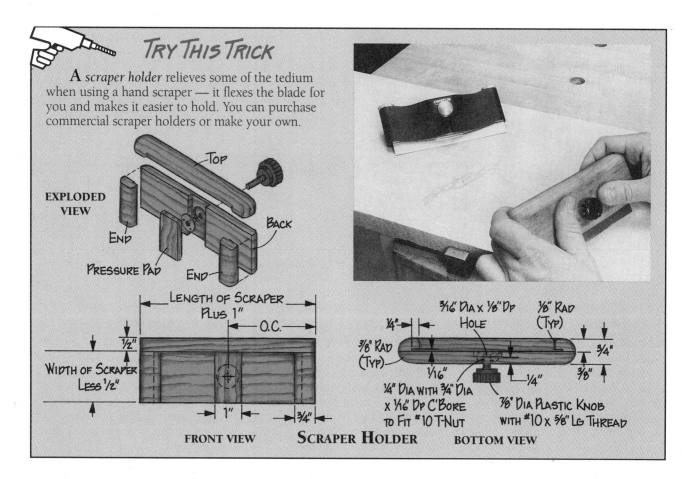

SHAPING

SHAPING PLANES

Although most hand planes are designed to cut flat surfaces, there are some made to create contoured shapes.

Molding planes cut single shapes — coves, beads, ogees, crown moldings, bed moldings, and so on. The sole and the plane iron are cut and ground to a negative of the profile they are designed to cut, as are router and shaper cutters. Oftentimes, the sole also incorporates a ledge that serves as a fence or a depth stop to guide or limit the cut. The irons are bedded at 55 to 60 degrees, a steeper angle than most planes. This helps reduce chipping and tearing when planing figured wood.

Many molding planes are designed to be canted at an angle as you cut with them, rather than to be held vertically. The cant angle is referred to as the *spring*. The spring does three things — it helps the craftsman hold the plane firmly against the edge of a board, it prevents tear-out at the corners, and it helps the plane clear the shavings.

Match planes are molding planes that cut mating shapes, such as rule joints or tongue-and-groove joints. *Panel-raising planes* (also called fielding planes) are molding planes that cut a wide shape and reduce the thickness at the edge of the panel so it will fit a groove. (*See Figure 4-25.*)

Both a *hollow plane* and a *compass plane* cut inside (concave) curves. The difference is that the curve of a hollow plane runs from side to side, while that of a compass plane runs front to back. Additionally, the sole of a compass plane is adjustable, allowing you to change the radius of the cut. (*See Figure 4-26.*)

Combination planes are designed to cut several different shapes — steps, beads, coves, V-shaped grooves, and round-bottom grooves. These can be used in combination to create more complex shapes. They will also cut simple joinery such as rabbets, dadoes, tongues, and grooves. Combination planes use interchangeable cutters and have adjustable fences and depth stops. (*See Figure 4-27.*)

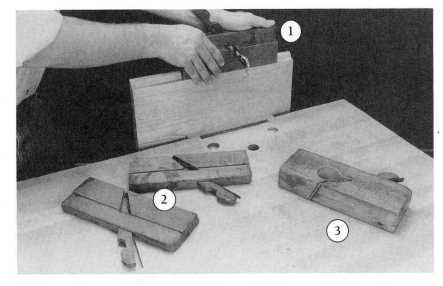

4-25 Three types of planes are designed to cut molded profiles in the ends and edges of boards. A *molding plane* (1) cuts both simple and complex shapes, depending on the design of the cutter and the sole. *Match planes* (2) cut mating negative and positive shapes, such as the mating cove and bead of a rule joint. A *panel-raising plane* (3) not only cuts a shape but also reduces the thickness of the board at the edge to fit a groove.

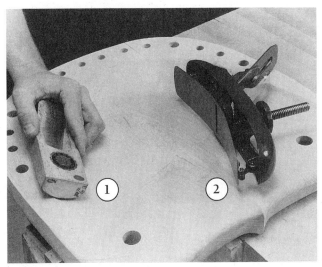

4-26 A *hollow plane* (1) has a fixed radius side to side to plow a wide, round-bottomed groove. Some also have a radius front to back, which make them handy for scooping chair seats and large bowls. A *compass plane* (2) cuts a concave or convex surface, the radius of which can be controlled by adjusting the curvature of the flexible metal sole. This is useful when making large architectural moldings.

4-27 A *combination plane* uses interchangeable cutters to create a variety of shapes and joints. An adjustable fence and depth stop guide the plane and let you cut to a precise depth.

SCRATCH STOCKS AND BEADERS

You can also scrape a contoured profile in wood, using a small scraper blade ground to a negative of the profile you want to cut. There are two tools designed to do this — a *scratch stock* and a *beading tool*. A scratch stock is designed to be held in one hand and is used like a marking gauge. A beading tool looks like a spokeshave and is pushed or pulled with two hands. (*See Figure 4-28.*)

4-28 A beading tool (or beader)
scrapes a profile in a board, using
small, interchangeable scraper blades.
Set the blade to the desired depth of
cut and adjust the fence to guide the
beader. Start by making very shallow
cuts, using only light pressure. With
each pass, the blade will scrape away
a little stock, cutting the profile a
little deeper. As the cut progresses,
it will become easier to guide the
beader and you can begin using a
little more pressure. If the blade chat-
ters or the cut looks ragged, ease up;
you're applying too much pressure.

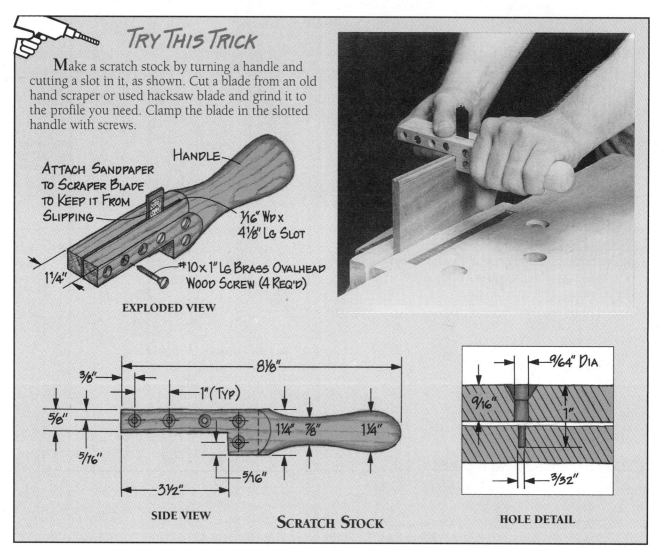

TRY THIS TRICK

Make a scratch stock by turning a handle and
cutting a slot in it, as shown. Cut a blade from an old
hand scraper or used hacksaw blade and grind it to
the profile you need. Clamp the blade in the slotted
handle with screws.

ATTACH SANDPAPER
TO SCRAPER BLADE
TO KEEP IT FROM
SLIPPING

HANDLE

¹⁄₁₆" WD x
4¹⁄₈" LG SLOT

#10 x 1" LG BRASS OVALHEAD
WOOD SCREW (4 REQ'D)

1¼"

EXPLODED VIEW

8¹⁄₈"

3⁄8"

1" (TYP)

5⁄8"

5⁄16"

1¼" 7⁄8" 1¼"

5⁄16"

3½"

SIDE VIEW

SCRATCH STOCK

9⁄64" DIA

9⁄16"

1"

3⁄32"

HOLE DETAIL

SHARPENING PLANES AND SCRAPERS

SHARPENING A PLANE IRON

The first time you sharpen a plane iron, grind the back perfectly flat and polish the surface. Thereafter, you shouldn't have to touch the back except to polish it — otherwise the blade will become too thin. Grind and hone the bevel *only*, then polish both the bevel and the back to remove the wire edge (the small burr that develops on the cutting edge).

Most plane irons are sharpened at 25 degrees. Use a slightly smaller angle for softwood and a slightly larger angle for hardwood and heavy-duty work. The precise angle isn't critical; many experienced crafts-men simply know how long the bevels on their plane irons should appear and sharpen them accordingly.

The shape of the cutting edge is more critical. To get the flattest possible surface, the edge should be straight across. Some craftsmen round the corners of smooth and jack plane irons to keep them from leaving ridges. But the irons of try planes, or any plane used for jointing, should be precisely square. If you use a plane for scrubbing or roughing cuts, grind the edge so it has a *slight* crown. This helps remove stock quickly. (*SEE FIGURE 4-29.*)

4-29 Sharpen a plane iron at 25 degrees for general-purpose work. If you work mostly with softwoods, *decrease* the angle by 2 or 3 degrees; if you work mostly with hardwoods or use the plane constantly, *increase* the angle by 2 or 3 degrees. For most planing operations, grind the bevel straight across, square to the sides of the plane iron. For smoothing and general planing, round the corners slightly — this prevents the plane iron from cutting ridges or steps in a planed surface. Leave the corners square if you use the plane for jointing or truing surfaces. If you have con-verted an old plane to a scrub plane or you use it mostly for roughing cuts, grind the bevel so it has a *slight* crown to help remove stock quickly.

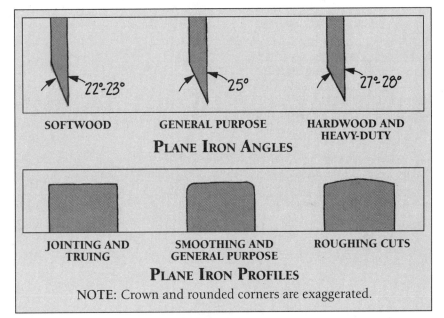

SOFTWOOD — 22°-23°
GENERAL PURPOSE — 25°
HARDWOOD AND HEAVY-DUTY — 27°-28°

PLANE IRON ANGLES

JOINTING AND TRUING
SMOOTHING AND GENERAL PURPOSE
ROUGHING CUTS

PLANE IRON PROFILES

NOTE: Crown and rounded corners are exaggerated.

A BIT OF ADVICE

Sharpen your plane irons the same way you might prepare a wood surface for a fine finish. Start with a coarse abrasive to grind the cutting edge, removing any nicks. Then work your way up through progressively finer abrasives to *polish* the surface. A polished edge will cut much better than one that's simply been ground. Use a honing guide to keep the bevel angle constant as you move from stone to stone.

SHARPENING A SCRAPER

To sharpen a scraper, you must raise burrs all along the edges of the tool. First, remove the old, dull burrs, filing and grinding the edges square. Then raise new burrs with a burnisher, rolling them over at the proper angle. (SEE FIGURES 4-30 THROUGH 4-33.)

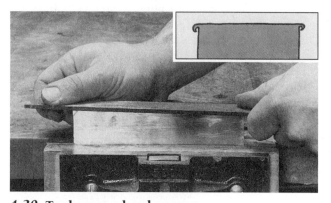

4-30 To sharpen a hand scraper, first file the edges square to the face of the blade with a second-cut (medium) mill file. The file will create small *wire edges* on the scraper as you joint it. Some craftsmen use these wire edges to scrape with, rather than going through the entire procedure of raising burrs. This works well, but the wire edges don't last as long as a true burr.

4-31 After filing, hone the edges with a medium sharpening stone. Then wipe the faces on the stone to remove any traces of the old burrs and the wire edges left by the file.

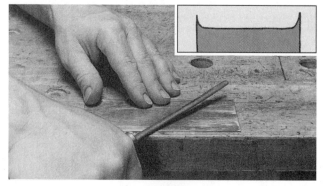

4-32 Place the scraper flat on your workbench. Lubricate the burnisher by rubbing it with a candle or paraffin. Draw the waxed burnisher toward you in one long stroke, pressing down hard enough that the burnisher makes a loud tick when it falls off the end of the scraper onto the workbench. Make a second stroke, pushing the burnisher away from you. Turn the scraper over and repeat. This will raise or *consolidate* a burr on each edge.

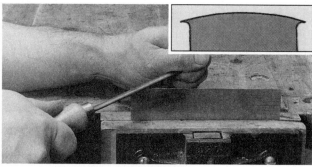

4-33 Clamp the scraper in a vise with the edge facing up. Cant the burnisher 10 to 15 degrees off horizontal and draw it along the edge, pressing down firmly. Then tilt the burnisher in the other direction and draw it along the edge again. Turn the scraper over and repeat for the other edge. This will roll the burrs over so they are between 75 and 80 degrees from the face. **Note:** This technique creates multiple cutting burrs on a scraper. When one wears out, switch to another.

ALIGNING AND ADJUSTING PLANES AND SCRAPERS

TUNING A HAND PLANE

While most good-quality hand planes work well just as they come from the manufacturer, some can benefit from a little judicious tuning. This is not the big deal that some craftsmen make it out to be; planes rarely have to be rebuilt. Like any other tool, they simply require some alignment and adjustment.

Make sure the back of the blade — the surface that faces down — is perfectly flat. Then check that it rests securely in the plane without rocking. If it does rock,

file the frog or the bed flat. (SEE FIGURE 4-34.) Also flatten the sole, if necessary, so the plane will cut true. (SEE FIGURE 4-35.) If the plane has a chip breaker, make sure the leading edge contacts the plane iron all across the width. (SEE FIGURE 4-36.) Finally, remove all the burrs and other imperfections from the cast metal parts. Most important, file a tiny chamfer all around the sole. This will prevent the edge from scratching the wood. (SEE FIGURE 4-37.)

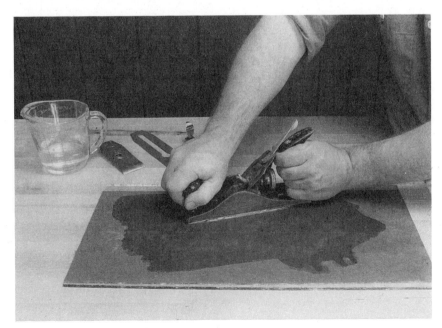

4-34 **Check that the back of your** plane iron is flat by laying it on a flat surface (such as the work surface of your jointer) and seeing if it rocks. If it does, grind it flat on a sharpening stone. Then check that the iron rests solidly on the frog or the supporting bed in the plane body. If the iron rocks, file the support flat. Don't be too aggressive when you do this; often all that's needed is one or two strokes of the file to remove a tiny burr or a bit of paint.

4-35 **A plane will only cut as true** as its sole. Check the flatness of the sole the same way you checked the back of the iron — rest it on a jointer table. If you see any daylight between the plane and the jointer, grind the sole flat. Affix wet/dry sandpaper to a large ¼-inch-thick plate of glass with contact cement. Using water to float away the metal filings, rub the plane back and forth until the sole is uniformly gray. (A shiny spot indicates an area on the sole that's not yet flat.) Start with 120-grit paper and finish with 320-grit or finer. **Note:** Remove the plane iron but leave the frog (if there is one) when you grind the sole. Otherwise, the sole may be stressed and pulled out of true when you tighten the screws that hold the frog in place.

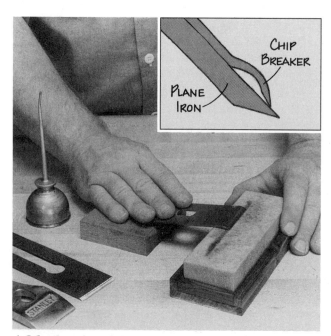

4-36 The edge of the chip breaker,
if there is one, should contact the
entire width of the plane iron with
no visible gaps. If the chip breaker
doesn't fit correctly after you flatten
the back of the iron, grind the edge
straight on a sharpening stone, as
shown. Note that most of the chip
breaker is off the stone and *lower*
than the edge that's being ground —
this creates the proper angle. You will
ruin the chip breaker if you grind it
with the body on the stone.

4-37 Remove any burrs, flashing,
or other imperfections from the cast
metal parts. Polish the surface of the
cam in the lever cap with Scotch-
Brite to make it smooth, and clean up
the edge of the mouth with a file, if
necessary. (Be careful *not* to widen
the mouth, however.) Most important, relieve the hard edges of the
sole, filing a tiny chamfer all around
the perimeter. This will keep the
edge of the sole from scratching or
marring the wood.

STORING AND LUBRICATING PLANES AND SCRAPERS

Protect the cutting edges when storing a hand plane.
You don't want to retract the blade every time you put
the plane away; it's hard enough to adjust it correctly.
Instead, cover the shelves where you store the planes
with felt, leather, or rubber. You can also secure small
wooden blocks to the shelves to prop up the ends of
the planes and hold the cutting edges off the surface.

When using a hand plane, get in the habit of
resting it on its side. The blade won't be damaged if
you rest it on a wood surface, but most workbenches
are cluttered with tools, hardened glue beads, and
sanding grit. These *will* hurt the cutting edge if you
happen to put the plane down on them.

. To lubricate a hand plane and protect it from rust,
wax and buff the metal parts, especially the sole. This
helps the plane to glide across the wood and seals the
metal surfaces from the effects of moisture.

TRY THIS TRICK

Keep a piece of felt, leather, or rubber spread
out on a corner of your workbench. Rest your hand
planes, handsaws, scrapers, chisels, and other cutting
tools on this soft material while you're working with
them. This will protect all your cutting edges.

5

Drilling and Boring

Since the earliest days of woodworking, the basic technique for boring a hole has remained the same. Ancient craftsmen spun long, straight sticks tipped with stone by rubbing their hands together, as an ordinary stick was spun against a piece of wood to start a fire. Today's craftsmen still spin bits to cut holes; only the designs of the bits and the methods used to spin them have changed.

The first drills known to have cutting edges were *spoon bits* used by the Romans. These were attached to simple handles that stuck out on either side, forming T-shaped *augers*. Sometime in the fifteenth century, medieval craftsmen began to use the cranklike *brace* to turn the bits, an innovation they probably imported from China.

At the end of the eighteenth century, the first twisted *auger bits* appeared. These were spiral blades that screwed themselves into the wood, lifting out the chips as they did so. Almost immediately, craftsmen began to fit them to braces, a combination that became the traditional *brace and bit*. About the time of the Civil War, Americans invented the gear-driven *hand drill* and a little later, the screw-driven *push drill*. During this same period, many new bits appeared, including some that were later adapted for use with electric drills — the brad-point bit, Forstner bit, and metal-cutting twist bit.

HAND DRILLS AND BITS

DRILLING AND BORING TOOLS

Although the portable electric drill has eclipsed most hand-powered drilling devices, three tools — the brace and bit, the hand drill, and the push drill — remain in general use today.

Braces — In the nineteenth century, craftsmen could choose from dozens of brace patterns fashioned from wood or metal. Today, most braces are metal, copied from a single popular design known as the American Pattern brace, or *joiner's brace*. (*SEE FIGURE 5-1.*) These have a rectangular steel frame, a rotating head and grip, and a "shell" chuck with a tapered mouth and two locking jaws. (*SEE FIGURE 5-2.*) This chuck is designed to accept bits with wedge-shaped *tangs* on the ends. These tangs are manufactured to a common Morse taper, making the bits interchangeable. (In 1861, Stephen A. Morse, a drill manufacturer, published a table of standardized tapers that is still used in toolmaking today.) A few manufacturers make braces with special four-jawed chucks that will grip both tang-end and round-shanked bits. Both types of chucks are designed to be tightened or loosened with your hand.

The brace operates like a crank. The grip is displaced horizontally from the head so you can swing it around and around. (*SEE FIGURE 5-3.*) The horizontal distance from the head to the grip is the *throw,* while the circle described by the grip as you turn it is the *sweep.* Braces usually have a sweep of 6 to 12 inches — the most common joiner's brace has a 10-inch sweep. The larger the sweep, the easier it is to turn the bit, especially when boring through hardwood. However, a *short brace* (a brace with a small sweep) is sometimes useful for working in tight spots.

Some braces have a ratchet at the foot to help you work in tight spaces where you can't make a full sweep. With the ratchet locked, you can turn the bit

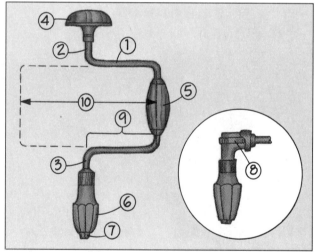

5-1 A typical *joiner's brace* has a rectangular metal *frame* (1) with a *neck* (2) and a *foot* (3), a rotating hardwood *head* (4) and *grip* (5), and a universal *shell chuck* (6) with locking *jaws* (7) that will accept auger bits with tapered tangs on the ends. Some braces have *ratchets* (8) at the foot to help you work in tight spaces. The horizontal distance the grip is displaced from the head is called the *throw* (9), while the circle described by the grip as you swing it around is the *sweep* (10).

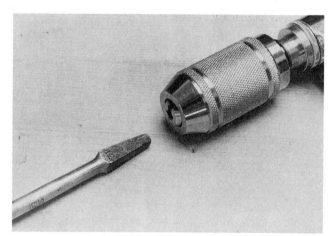

5-2 The *shell chuck,* or Barber chuck, as it was called when introduced in 1864, was a major step forward in drilling tools. Before then, every manufacturer had a different mechanism to mount a bit in a brace. (Some had two or three.) Consequently, if you needed several types of bits, you might have to purchase several braces to use them. The Barber chuck was designed to accept a bit with a standard-size tapered *tang* on the end. Soon, almost all braces were made with Barber chucks and bits were forged with interchangeable tangs.

clockwise and counterclockwise just as you would
with a normal brace. When you release the ratchet,
however, you can only turn the bit in one direction.
This allows you to bore a hole making partial sweeps.
A *joist brace* — a brace with a ratchet head, similar
to a ratchet wrench — lets you work in more confined areas (such as the space between joists) where
there isn't room for a full sweep or a long brace. (*See
Figure 5-4.*)

   Hand drills — The hand drill, or wheel brace, as it
was originally called, uses two beveled gears to turn
the bit. The larger of the two gears (the wheel) is
mounted vertically so it can be turned by a crank. It
engages a smaller gear at the top of a chuck. The ratio
between the two gears varies, but on average, a single
revolution of the wheel produces about ten revolu-
tions of the chuck. This allows you to spin the bit
much faster than you can with a brace and bit. (*See
Figures 5-5 and 5-6.*)

A BIT OF ADVICE

Although many craftsmen reach for a power
drill when they have a tough job that requires a lot
of muscle, this isn't always the best choice. When
boring holes in thick hardwood, a brace and bit
will do a better job in less time. And, in most
cases, you'll expend less energy.

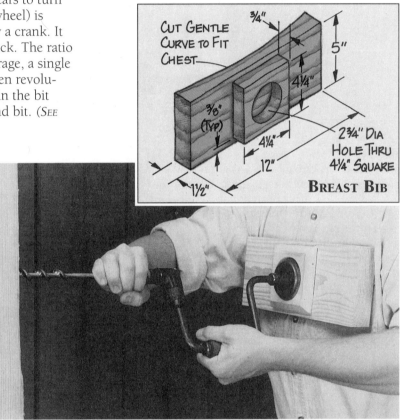

CUT GENTLE CURVE TO FIT CHEST

3/4"
5"
4¼"
3/8" (TYP)
4¼"
12"
1½"
2¾" DIA HOLE THRU 4¼" SQUARE

BREAST BIB

5-3 Use a brace like a crank,
swinging the grip round and round
to turn the bit. As you do so, apply
steady pressure to the head to feed
the bit into the wood. You can use
your chest to feed the bit — this is
less tiring than using your arm. If
you do a lot of work with a brace and
bit, consider making a **breast bib** to
protect your chest. In a thick piece of
wood, cut a gentle curve to fit your
chest comfortably. Bore a hole in a
small scrap to hold the head of the
brace, and glue it to the flat face of
the thick board. When working,
place the bib between your chest
and the brace — the pressure will
hold it in place.

5-4 To use a brace and bit to bore
a hole, you must have enough
working room for both the sweep
and the length of the brace. When
working in confined spaces where
you don't have room for either, use a
joist brace. This brace has no frame.
Instead, there is a ratchet and a
chuck immediately under the head,
and a handle that sticks out horizontally from the ratchet. Turn the bit by
moving the handle back and forth.
Note: A joist brace also gives you
more leverage when boring through
extremely hard woods.

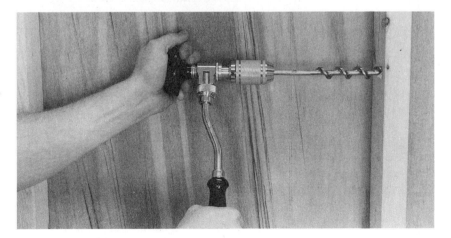

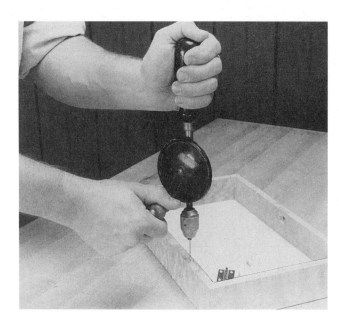

5-5 To use a hand drill, simply
hold the tool by its vertical handle
and turn the crank. Because it's
designed to drill small holes, usually
only gentle pressure is required to
feed the bit. For those operations
where more pressure is needed, some
hand drills have an extra handle
mounted horizontally, opposite the
crank. Grip the horizontal handle
and press against the vertical handle
with your chest, in the same manner
you would press against the head of a
brace. **Note:** A *breast drill* is a large
hand drill occasionally used by carpenters to bore holes in timbers. This
drill has a breast plate in place of the
vertical handle.

The hand drill supplements the capabilities of a
brace and bit. Because of the way in which an auger
bit cuts the wood, it's difficult to manufacture one
smaller than ¼ inch in diameter. But hand drills are
made to hold ordinary round-shanked twist bits,
allowing you to bore holes as small as ¹⁄₁₆ inch in
diameter. With a special *zero-clearance chuck,* you
can use *wire gauge drills* to make even smaller holes.

Push drills — Old-time craftsmen sometimes used
Archimedean drills to bore small holes. These tools
had spiral shafts and a "travelling" handle that slid up
and down the shaft, causing it to spin. Late in the
nineteenth century, tool manufacturers enclosed the
shaft and added a spring to return the travelling
handle after each stroke. The improved tool became
known as a push drill.

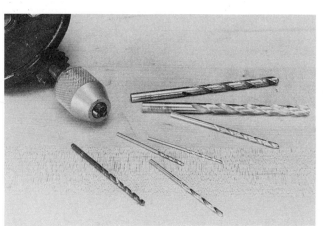

5-6 A hand drill has a three-jawed
chuck, much like the chucks on
portable electric drills and drill
presses. This lets you mount small
round-shanked bits.

TRY THIS TRICK

Use a hand drill as a nail spinner. Before ham-
mering a nail into thin or brittle stock, cut off the
head of a nail that size and mount it in the drill
chuck. Spin the nail into the wood, boring a pilot
hole to prevent splitting the stock.

The advantage of the push drill over other hand-
powered drilling tools is that it only requires one
hand to operate it. Simply place the tip of the bit
where you want to bore a hole and push down on the
handle several times. (*See Figure 5-7.*)

HAND DRILL BITS

By the end of the 1800s, there was a wide selection
of bits for hand boring, especially tang-end bits to fit
a brace. However, since the advent of power drills,

the selection has been much reduced. You can still find many useful bits in flea markets, but if you want to purchase new bits, there are only a few types commonly available.

Auger bits have a spiral body to lift the wood chips out of the hole as you work. Two types of spiral bodies are commonly available (*SEE FIGURE 5-8*):

■ A *double-twist body* is made from a flat sheet of tool steel that is twisted to form a spiral. Both edges coil around the axis of the bit, hence the "double" twist.

■ A *solid-center body* has a solid stem running down the center with a spiral fin wound around it. The stem reinforces the fin, making this design much stronger than the double-twist body.

Additionally, the cutting ends of the bits — the *noses* — can be different. There are also two different types of nose patterns commonly available (also shown in Figure 5-8):

■ A *Scotch nose* has a flat cutting edge across the bottom of the bit, *wings* to cut the side of the hole, and a threaded point or *screw lead* to center the bit and help draw it through the wood. This design is best used for boring hardwoods and doing rough construction work.

■ A *Jennings nose* (designed by Russell Jennings in 1855) has a flat cutting edge and a screw lead like

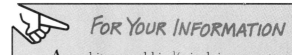

the Scotch nose, but it uses protruding *spurs* on either side of the cutting edge to cut the sides of the hole. It will bore cleaner holes than a Scotch nose and is better suited for fine woodworking.

Spoon bits have a spoonlike nose with sharp cutting edges. The gouge-shaped body may be tapered or straight. Typically, spoon bits will bore cleaner holes with smoother sides than auger bits. For this reason, these ancient drilling tools are still preferred by traditional chairmakers for making round mortises. (*SEE FIGURE 5-9*.)

Drill points come with most push drills. These are small bits, under ¼ inch in diameter, with straight cutting edges or *flutes*. The shanks are designed specifically to fit a push drill chuck. (*SEE FIGURE 5-10*.)

Twist bits and other ordinary round-shanked bits, such as brad-point bits and high-speed bits, can

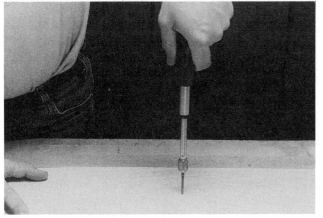

5-7 A *push drill* uses a "spiral ratchet drive" to spin a drill bit. As you push on the handle, it slides down a spiral shaft, causing the shaft to rotate. A spring returns the handle for the next push. A ratchet between the shaft and the chuck prevents the bit from spinning backward on the return stroke. **Note:** Many push drills have compartments in the handles to hold bits.

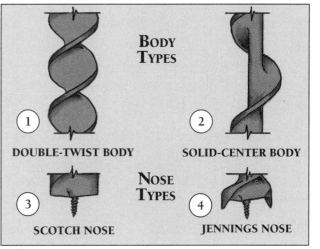

5-8 Auger bits are available with different types of bodies and noses. A *double-twist body* (1) is best suited for light duty, while a *solid-center body* (2) will stand up to heavier work. A *Scotch nose* (3) is designed to bore rough holes in hard woods, while a *Jennings nose* (4) is preferred for fine woodworking.

be used in hand drills if they aren't too large for the chuck.

Additionally, there are a few unique bits for hand drilling tools with special applications (SEE FIGURE 5-11):

■ An *expansion bit* has a screw lead and an expandable cutting edge that can be used to bore large holes between 1 and 3 inches in diameter.

■ A *countersink bit* has tapered flutes to cut countersinks for flathead wood screws.

■ A *screwdriver bit* looks like an ordinary screwdriver but has a tang, rather than a handle, on the end of its shaft. It's especially effective for driving large screws into hard materials, where a good deal of torque is required.

5-9 Because spoon bits bore a cleaner hole than auger bits, some craftsmen prefer them for making round mortises. To use a spoon bit, you must first gouge a small depression in the wood where you want to drill the hole. This helps center the bit and keeps it from wandering when you start boring. As you work, stop every few minutes and blow the chips out of the hole. Unlike an auger bit, a spoon bit does not automatically clear the chips.

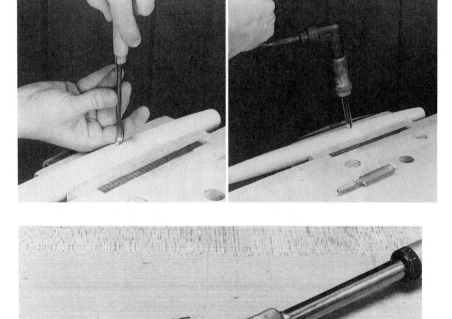

5-10 The chuck on a push drill tends to be a simple affair with a spring-loaded ball-bearing latch rather than locking jaws. Consequently, it will not mount standard tang-end or round-shanked bits. Instead, the tool usually comes with a set of straight-fluted bits, called *drill points.* These have grooves in the shanks to engage the latch. They can also be mounted in hand drills.

①

②

③

5-11 In addition to ordinary drill bits, there are a few special-purpose bits for hand operations. Use an adjustable *expansion bit* (1) to bore large holes between 1 and 3 inches in diameter. Ream out countersinks for flathead screws with a *countersink bit* (2). And a *screwdriver bit* (3) mounted in a brace reduces the effort required to drive large screws through hard materials.

DRILLING ACCESSORIES

In addition to tools for boring holes, there are also a couple of hand drilling accessories for shooting screws (*SEE FIGURE 5-12*):

■ A *gimlet* is a miniature auger. This T-shaped hand tool has a screw tip to start a hole and a spiral shaft to ream it out. Use it to start screws in softwood, where you don't need to bore a deep pilot hole. These tools are difficult to find new, but they are still plentiful at flea markets.

■ A *hand countersink* is a countersink bit mounted in its own handle. Use it to sink the heads of flathead screws. It's handy when you're just shooting a few screws or when you need to remove the burrs around the edge of a hole.

5-12 Two hand drilling accessories are useful when shooting screws: A *gimlet* (1) is a miniature auger that bores starter holes for screws. A *hand countersink* (2) reams out a screw hole to create a sink for the screw head.

CARING FOR DRILLING TOOLS

SHARPENING

When an auger bit becomes dull or no longer cuts well, you must sharpen both the cutting edges and the spurs (or wings, depending on the nose pattern). To do this, you need an *auger bit file,* a small tapered file that allows you to work on both wide and narrow surfaces. It's also handy to have a small *slipstone* or a *ceramic file* to hone the surfaces. (*SEE FIGURE 5-13.*)

Sharpen the spurs first, filing the *inside* surfaces. (*SEE FIGURE 5-14.*) Check that both spurs are the same length. Then file the leading faces of the cutting edges, making sure the edges are parallel. (*SEE FIGURE 5-15.*) If the bit has wings rather than spurs, file these sharp the same way you filed the cutting edges, then hone them still sharper.

Finally, check the lead screw. If the threads are bent or pinched, true them with a small triangular file. Remove as little metal as possible, but enough to open the valleys between the threads.

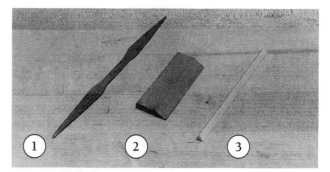

5-13 To sharpen an auger bit, you need an *auger bit file* (1). One end of this small, tapered file has safe edges while the other has safe faces. (A *safe* file surface has no teeth.) This lets you sharpen edges without cutting into adjacent surfaces on the bit. After filing, use a *slipstone* (2) or a *ceramic file* (3) to hone the cutting edges.

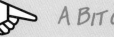

A BIT OF ADVICE

Never, ever touch the *outside* surfaces of a bit with a file or a sharpening stone, except to remove burrs. This will change the shape and the diameter of the bit, causing it to cut unevenly and bind in the hole.

5-14 Secure the auger bit in a vise and file the *inside* surfaces of the spurs. Be careful to file the entire surface, applying even pressure. If you file just the tip or press too hard against the top of the spur, the spur will eventually become too thick at the base. When you have finished sharpening the spurs, make sure they are the same length. Twist the screw lead into a flat board, holding the bit perpendicular to the surface. Both spurs should begin to cut at the same time. If they don't, file the longer spur even with the other.

5-15 After sharpening the spurs, file the *leading faces* of the cutting edges — the surfaces that face up as you bore a hole. Filing the trailing faces can interfere with the clearance angles, preventing the bit from cutting properly and making it difficult to turn. Hold the bit in a vise, as shown, and file the edges so the bevel angle will be about 30 degrees. The precise angle is not critical; close is good enough. Inspect the nose to make sure you have filed the edges parallel, then bore a test hole. If one cutting edge takes a thicker shaving than the other, that edge is too long. File the long edge back until the shavings are the same thickness.

STORAGE

When storing bits, protect the cutting edges as you would any other cutting tool. Don't just throw them in a drawer or a tool box where they can rattle around, bumping against one another. Hang them up, make a rack for them, or store them in a *bit roll* — a length of canvas with pouches sewed in it. (*See Figure 5-16.*) These pouches cover the cutting edges, and the canvas lets moisture evaporate that might otherwise collect on the metal surfaces.

5-16 Store your auger bits and other hand drilling accessories in a canvas *bit roll.* The pouches cover the individual cutting edges and prevent them from bumping into one another, even when you tote your bits from job to job. The cloth also lets moisture evaporate quickly, keeping the bits from rusting. Avoid leather and plastic rolls; these don't "breathe" well, and moisture may collect inside them.

6

CUTTING AND CHOPPING

There are no simpler hand tools than chisels and knives; in effect, these are just blades mounted on the ends of sticks. Despite this simplicity (or perhaps because of it), they are incredibly versatile. With a small selection of chisels and knives, you can create almost any shape in wood — this, after all, is what carvers do. But these tools are also invaluable in general woodworking for a variety of operations — shaving surfaces, fitting joints, adjusting shapes and profiles, cutting mortises, marking cuts, removing glue beads, sharpening pencils — the list is almost endless.

Metal chisels and knives have been used since the Bronze Age; archaeologists have found stone molds that were used for casting them. The Romans developed several kinds of chisels for specific woodworking tasks, including *firmer* and *mortise* chisels, which we still use today. Medieval craftsmen began to bevel the edges of chisels to work in tight spots. (Before then, this work had to be accomplished with thin-bladed knives.) In the eighteenth century,

advances included riveted handles for knives and turned handles with hoops and ferrules for chisels.

In the nineteenth century, this evolution culminated in the "registered" chisel — a heavy-duty, general-purpose firmer chisel with an exceptionally strong blade, bolster, turned hardwood handle, ferrule, hoop, and a leather washer that acted as a shock absorber between the blade and the handle. Just who registered this design has been forgotten, but it has remained a standard of quality among hand tools for over a century.

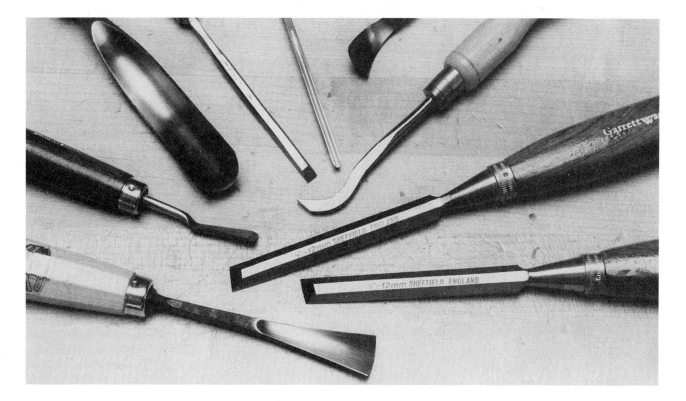

USING CHISELS, GOUGES, AND KNIVES

TYPES OF CHISELS

There are two ways to mount a chisel blade to a handle. Some blades are forged with a long, tapered *tang* on the back end, with the tang forced into a hole in the handle. Others are made with a *socket* on the back and a handle shaped to fit the socket. The problem with both arrangements is that the wooden handle eventually compresses or splits, and the blade becomes loose. To forestall the inevitable, tool manufacturers forge a *bolster* on a tanged blade to prevent the tang from splitting the handle. They may also install a metal ring or *ferrule* around the front of the handle to reinforce it. If the chisel is designed to be hit with a mallet, a *hoop* or a *leather tip* on the back end keeps the handle from mushrooming, and a *leather washer* between the handle and the bolster (or the handle and the socket) cushions the blows and keeps the metal blade from compressing the softer wood. (*SEE FIGURE 6-1.*)

Regardless of how it's mounted, the blade is a rectangular piece of tool steel with a cutting edge on the front or *nose*. The cutting edge is ground so there is a *bevel* on one face only; the opposite face (or *back*) is flat. The edges may also be beveled to help you work in corners that are less than 90 degrees, but these bevels are never ground to a cutting edge. This would make the blade dangerous to hold. The length, width, and thickness of a blade — and whether or not the edges are beveled — determine the purpose of a chisel.

There are four types of chisels with flat blades, ranging from ⅛ to 2 inches wide (*SEE FIGURE 6-2*):

■ A *paring chisel* has a long, thin blade that is lighter than other chisels. This chisel is designed to be pushed with your hands; the thin blade may snap with a heavy blow from a mallet. It almost always has beveled edges and is used for fine trimming and fitting.

■ A *firmer chisel* (sometimes called a framing chisel) has a slightly heavier blade, thick enough to withstand the shock from mallet blows. It may or may not have beveled edges and will work well for a wide range of cutting operations. (*SEE FIGURE 6-3.*)

■ A *mortise chisel* has a stout, thick blade, sometimes thicker than it is wide. The blade and the handle will withstand repeated heavy blows from a mallet. This chisel is used for cutting mortises and other heavy work.

■ *Special-purpose chisels* are designed for specific woodworking tasks. These include skew, corner, drawer lock, dog leg, crank-neck, and swan-neck chisels, as well as many other chisels for carving and turning. (*SEE FIGURES 6-4 THROUGH 6-7.*)

6-1 A chisel *blade* (1) is a rectangular piece of steel with a *bevel* (2) and a *cutting edge* (3) ground on the *nose* (4). The blade may also have *beveled edges* (5). With a few exceptions, these bevels are ground on one surface only; the *back* (6) is left flat. The blade begins to taper at the *shoulder* (7) down to a narrow *neck* (8). The neck is joined to a *handle* (9) with a *tang* (10) or a *socket* (11). Tanged chisels often have a *bolster* (12) to stop the tang from splitting the handle. A *ferrule* (13) reinforces the handle where the tang is inserted. If the chisel is intended to be hit with a mallet, a *hoop* (14) or a *leather tip* (15) will keep the wood from mushrooming. There may also be a *leather washer* (16) between the blade and the handle to absorb the shock of each mallet blow.

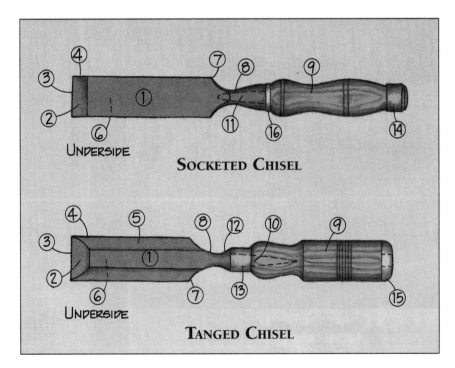

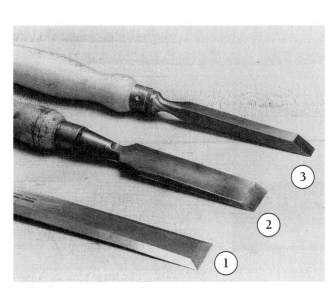

6-2 The three types of chisels designed for general woodworking tasks all have flat blades, ranging from ⅛ to 2 inches wide. They differ in blade length and thickness. A *paring chisel* (1) is a light-duty chisel with a long, thin blade, intended for trimming and fitting. It should not be hit with a mallet. A *firmer chisel* (2) has a shorter and thicker blade for medium-duty tasks. It can be tapped with a mallet. A *mortise chisel* (3) has an extremely thick blade to withstand heavy-duty work and repeated blows with a mallet.

6-3 A firmer chisel with beveled edges is often listed in catalogs as a "beveled-edge chisel." This is a versatile design; it can also be used as a paring chisel. It will not stand up to constant heavy-duty work, but if you take light cuts, you can make a mortise with it. If you only buy one set of chisels, this is your best choice.

6-4 Just as a beveled edge on a chisel blade lets you work up against surfaces that are less than 90 degrees from the surface you're cutting, an angled cutting edge (called a *skew*) lets you reach into corners that are less than 90 degrees. To reach all the surfaces in an acute corner, you'll need both a right and a left skew. A double skew can also be useful for some tasks. **Note:** You can easily grind your own skew chisels from worn-out straight chisels rather than pay the high price most manufacturers charge for this specialized grind.

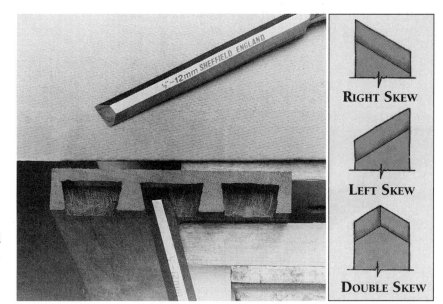

RIGHT SKEW

LEFT SKEW

DOUBLE SKEW

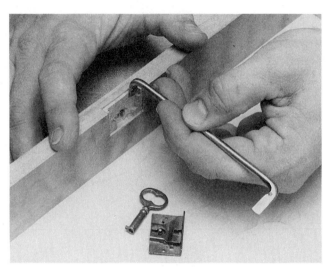

6-5 The blade of a *corner chisel* is very stout. The cutting edge forms a V-shape, as if two mortise chisels were joined at 90 degrees. Use it to square the corners of mortises. **Note:** A corner chisel is ground with the bevels *inside* the V, the technical term for which is an *in-cannel* grind. Because of this, it cannot be used to cut V-shaped grooves like a parting tool with an *out-cannel* grind (bevels on the outside). It's difficult to control the depth of cut; the inside bevels want to dig into the wood.

6-6 Once in a great while, you need a chisel to reach around corners. A *drawer lock chisel* does just that. The blade is bent 90 degrees just before the cutting edge. Some drawer lock chisels have no handle. Instead, each end of the blade has a cutting edge. One is bent down; the other is bent to the side.

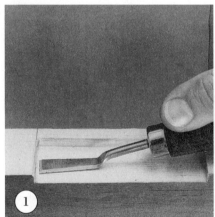

(1)

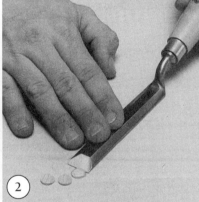

(2)

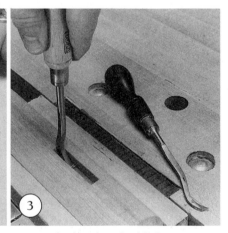

(3)

6-7 Several specialized chisels have bent blades, either to reach into recesses or to keep the handle above the wood as you work. A *dogleg chisel* (1) has a small blade, bent in the middle, and is handy for small paring jobs such as cleaning out hinge mortises. These chisels often have skewed cutting edges to reach

into corners. A *crank-neck chisel* (2) has a full-size blade bent at the neck so you can rest the blade back on the wood and cut flush to the surface in the middle of large, flat boards. You can also use it to trim the bottoms of dadoes and grooves. A *swan-neck chisel* (3) is a bent mortising chisel, designed to cut the bottoms of mor-

tises. The bend in the blade gives you the leverage you need. Rest the bend against the end of the mortise, press down on the nose, and use the handle like a lever. The sharp edge will scrape along the bottom of the recess, cutting it deeper.

FOR YOUR INFORMATION

How do you know whether you have a beveled-edge firmer chisel or a paring chisel? Look at the blade from the side. Paring chisels are long and thin; firmer chisels are somewhat shorter and thicker. Also study the handle. Is there a hoop or leather tip at the end or a leather washer between the handle and the blade? This indicates a firmer chisel that can be struck with a mallet. If you can't decide, you're probably not supposed to. Many tool manufacturers make sets of medium-duty chisels that walk the line between firmer and paring chisels.

USING A CHISEL

There are a few rules of thumb for cutting with a chisel that, with minor exceptions, apply to all types:

■ Use a chisel as both a cutting tool and a wedge. Cut the wood fibers or split them, as needed. (*See Figures 6-8 and 6-9.*)

■ Use the chisel with the bevel down when you need to control the depth of cut, and with the bevel up when you want to use the flat back to guide the tool. (*See Figures 6-10 and 6-11.*)

■ When using a mallet to drive a chisel, tap on the end of the handle; don't pound. (*See Figure 6-12.*)

■ To drive a chisel without a mallet, rely on the weight of your body, not your muscles, to push it forward. (*See Figure 6-13.*)

6-8 You can use a chisel as both a cutting tool and a wedge. For example, when removing the waste between dovetail pins, first cut down about ¹⁄₁₆ inch into the wood, severing the wood fibers along the baseline. Then split away a ¹⁄₁₆-inch-thick chip up to the baseline and lift it out. Repeat, cutting and splitting ¹⁄₁₆ inch at a time, until you have removed all the waste. **Note:** To make the cut surface as clean and flat as possible, always split away a little less wood than you cut. If you split away too much, you'll tear the uncut fibers and the surface will look ragged.

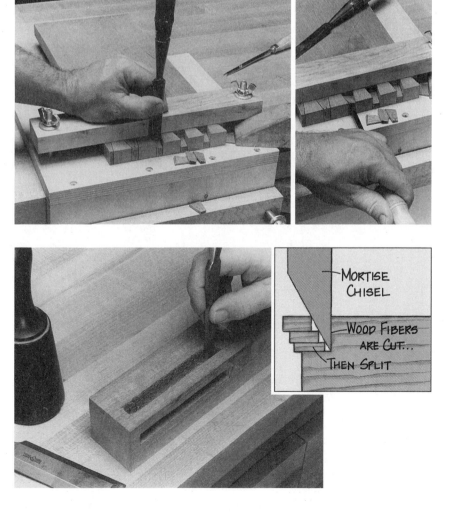

6-9 When cutting a mortise, use the mortise chisel as a cutter and a wedge *at the same time*. As you drive the cutting edge down through the wood, the blade severs the fibers while its bevel pushes the waste sideways and splits off the chips. **Note:** Don't remove more than ¹⁄₁₆ inch at a time from the mortise — the work will actually progress faster if you take smaller bites. When you try to cut away too much at one time, it's more difficult to split the waste, and the cut takes more time and effort.

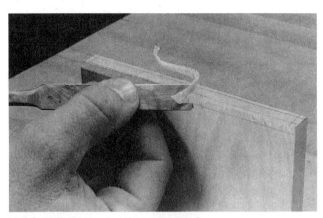

6-10 When you need to "steer" the chisel, cut with the bevel *down*. This lets you use the handle like a lever to adjust the cutting angle and the depth of cut. To cut deeper, raise the handle. For a shallower cut, lower it.

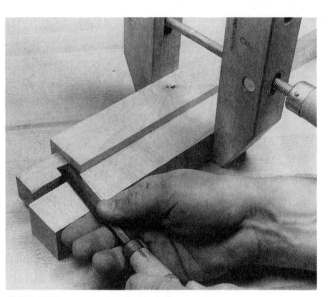

6-11 When you need to make a perfectly straight cut, use the back of the chisel to guide it. Rest the back on a flat surface and drive the chisel forward, holding the back against the surface as you do so. For some operations, you must clamp a block to the work, as shown, to provide a guide for the chisel.

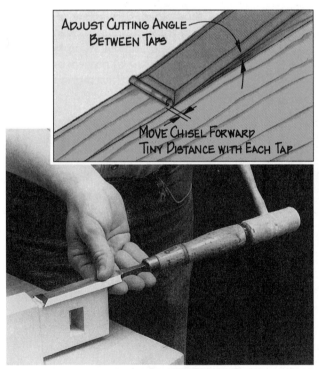

6-12 When using a mallet to drive a chisel, don't pound on the handle. It's difficult to control the chisel, and the exertion will wear you out. Additionally, a heavy glancing blow may chip the cutting edge. Instead, drive the chisel forward with light taps, adjusting the cutting angle as needed between each tap. If the chisel is sharp, the cut will proceed very quickly.

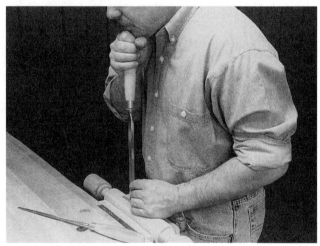

6-13 When driving a chisel with- out the aid of a mallet, use the weight of your body, not your muscles. Lean into the chisel or push on the handle with your chest, hip, even your chin. This technique is much less tiresome than trying to muscle a chisel through the wood. And surprisingly, it gives you more control, letting you use your muscles to steer or brake the chisel.

GOUGES

Gouges are "hollow" chisels, with blades that curve from edge to edge. Some of the distinctions that apply to chisels also hold for gouges. There are thin-bladed *paring gouges* designed for light work, and heavy-duty *firmer gouges* that can be driven with a mallet. The blades come in different widths, from 1/8 to 2 inches, the same as chisels.

Gouge blades are also distinguished by their radius or *sweep*. You can purchase a gouge with a very shallow or a very deep sweep. The different sweeps are numbered between #1 and #12 — the higher the number, the deeper the sweep. (*SEE FIGURE 6-14.*)

Gouge blades also come in several shapes, designed for different operations (*SEE FIGURE 6-15*):

■ A *straight gouge* has a long, straight pod with parallel edges — a hollow chisel. These are designed for general work in which you need a curved cutting edge.

■ A *fishtail gouge* tapers from a wide nose to a narrow neck. These are divided into two types — "long-pod" fishtail gouges have the same range of widths and sweeps as straight gouges, while "allongee" fishtail gouges are somewhat wider. (Both have long pods, however — go figure.) This is an oriental tool design, once known as a *Chinese gouge*. It's used for general work, like a straight gouge.

■ A *bent gouge* also has a long pod, but the pod is curved from front to back as well as edge to edge. From the side, it has a shape similar to a swan-neck chisel, with the cutting edge bent up. This bend helps you reach into recessed areas like bowls.

■ A *spoon gouge* has a short pod with a long neck. It's used mostly for fine detail work on concave surfaces.

■ A *back-bent gouge* is a short-pod spoon gouge with the blade bent down, in the opposite direction of a bent gouge. It's used for detail work on convex surfaces.

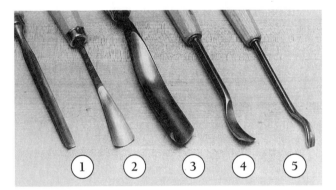

6-15 Gouges come in several shapes, each with different uses. A *straight gouge* (1) and a *fishtail gouge* (2) are for general work in which a curved blade is needed; a *bent gouge* (3) will reach into a recessed area; a *spoon gouge* (4) is for detail work on concave surfaces, while a *back-bent gouge* (5) is for convex surfaces.

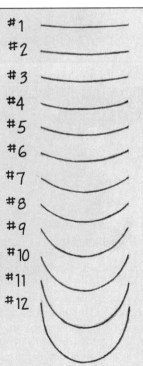

#1
#2
#3
#4
#5
#6
#7
#8
#9
#10
#11
#12

6-14 Gouges come in different widths and radii. The radius of the curved blade is known as the *sweep*, while the curved or *swept* portion of a gouge is the *pod*. Sweeps are numbered from #1 to #12 — the larger the sweep, the smaller the radius and the deeper the pod. The blades of #1 gouges have a large radius and a very shallow pod, while #12 gouges are much tighter and deeper. For practical purposes, few tool retailers offer a complete range of sweeps. They usually stock just the odd numbers, starting with #3 and ending with #11.

FOR YOUR INFORMATION

While most gouges have an out-cannel grind (a bevel on the outside of the curve), there are a few available with in-cannel grinds so the bevel is inside the curve. In-cannel gouges will cut in a straight line and are useful for cutting or trimming round-bottom grooves. Some have crank-necks to reach into long grooves.

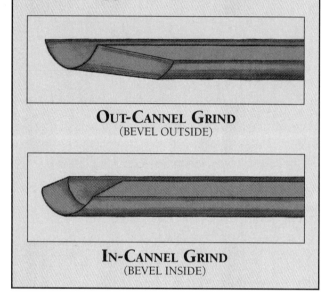

OUT-CANNEL GRIND
(BEVEL OUTSIDE)

IN-CANNEL GRIND
(BEVEL INSIDE)

OTHER SHAPES

In addition to the straight cutting edges of chisels and the curved edges of gouges, there are several other shapes available (*SEE FIGURE 6-16*):

■ A *veiner* is a thin, narrow gouge with a U-shaped cutting edge and an extremely deep pod for cutting round-bottom grooves.

■ A *fluter* is similar to a veiner, but it is wider and has a slightly shallower pod.

■ A *parting tool* has a V-shaped cutting edge for making V-grooves. It's available in different sizes and angles.

■ A *macaroni tool* cuts a square-bottom groove. The cutting edge is shaped like an open box with straight sides and square corners.

■ A *fluteroni tool* is similar to a macaroni tool, but the corners are slightly rounded.

KNIVES

The difference between a chisel and a knife is that a chisel cuts with its nose, while a knife cuts with its edge. There is not a great need for this sort of tool in a woodworking shop unless you do a lot of carving. However, it is a good idea to keep one or two around for detail work, scribing lines, and odd jobs. (*SEE FIGURES 6-17 AND 6-18.*)

6-16 In addition to straight chisels and curved gouges, there are other cutting tools with edges forged in a variety of shapes — *veiner* (1), *fluter* (2), *parting tool* (3), *macaroni tool* (4), and *fluteroni tool* (5). These are used mostly for carving or detail work.

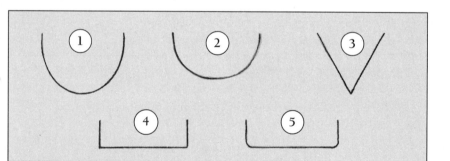

6-17 Although knives are not used much in general woodworking, they come in handy on occasion. Some craftsmen keep a *pocket knife* (1) or a *chip-carving knife* (2) in their tool boxes for trimming, paring, and other detail work. An *X-Acto tool* (3), with disposable blades, can also be used for this sort of work.

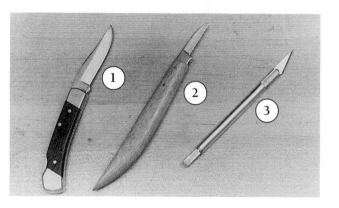

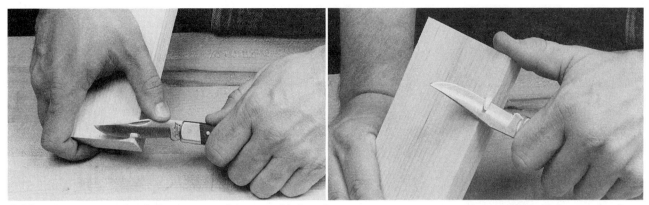

6-18 When using a knife for trimming and paring, hold the knife in one hand and place the thumb of your other hand against the back of the blade. Use your thumb as a fulcrum, pulling the handle of the knife back to move the blade forward, away from your body. When you must cut toward your body, grasp the handle with your fingers and hook your thumb over the end of the board to draw the knife toward you. **Warning:** Use your thumb *only* to pull the knife along; *do NOT* pull the knife with your arm muscles. If the wood splits and the knife loses its purchase, you could jab yourself in the chest. Besides, the thumb technique takes less force and gives you more control than trying to pull the blade through the wood with your arms.

TRY THIS TRICK

Use the point of a knife to help position small parts when gluing up a project.

ADZE

An *adze* is an ancient tool, similar to an axe but designed for smaller chopping tasks. In medieval times, it was a standard tool in every craftsman's tool kit, used for rough shaping or for dressing the surface of rough lumber before planing. Today, it's used by carvers for roughing out large shapes and by chairmakers for roughing out chair seats. (*SEE FIGURE 6-19.*)

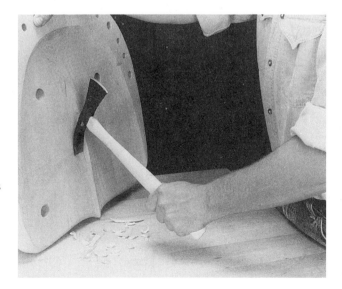

6-19 An *adze* looks like a hand axe and is used to chop rough shapes in wood. Often the cutting edge is perpendicular to the handle rather than parallel. There are two types — straight and curved. The small adze shown combines both a straight and a curved blade on a single head.

CARVING TOOLS

Woodcarvers have created many specialized chisels and knives for cutting three-dimensional shapes in wood. There are thousands of these tools — one manufacturer alone lists over 3,000 in its catalog! However, professional carvers rarely use more than 50 or so, depending on the type of objects they carve. Many experienced woodworkers keep an even smaller selection of carving tools on hand for occasional detail work.

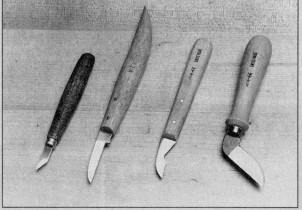

If you want to put together a basic set of carving chisels, those shown will handle almost every carving job that is likely to come up in a woodworking shop — a *small gouge* (1) with a medium sweep, a *large gouge* (2) with a large sweep, a *large bent gouge* (3) with a large sweep, a *medium-size parting tool* (4), a *small veiner* (5), and *right and left medium-size skew chisels* (6 and 7). Some manufacturers put together sets of "cabinetmaker's carving tools" with a selection of chisels similar to this.

A small selection of carving knives with different shapes of blades will also come in handy. Don't waste your money on a complete set. The four shown are your basic choices, and two or three of these are likely to be all you'll ever need.

CARING FOR CHISELS, GOUGES, AND KNIVES

SHARPENING

The bevels of most chisels, gouges, and similar cutting tools are sharpened at 25 to 30 degrees — slightly less for softwood, more for hardwood and heavy-duty work. The precise angle isn't critical, however, as long as you're within two or three degrees. What *is* important is that you hold the angle *precisely* as you grind, hone, and polish the bevel. To do this, use a honing guide. (*See Figures 6-20 and 6-21.*)

The first time you sharpen a chisel, grind and hone the back flat. Thereafter, only polish the back. (*See Figure 6-22.*) Grind, hone, and polish the bevel, working your way up through progressively finer abrasives. (*See Figure 6-23.*) Remove the burr or *wire edge* that develops on the bevel by alternately polishing the bevel and the back on the finest stone. (*See Figure 6-24.*) If you wish to put a *microbevel* on the cutting edge, increase the sharpening angle 3 to 5 degrees and make several passes over the finest stone. (*See Figure 6-25.*)

6-20 Many woodworkers inadver-
tently rock the chisel slightly as they
move it back and forth over a sharpening stone. Or, they change angles
slightly as they switch from coarser
stones to finer ones. Both of these
oversights can ruin your cutting
edge. To keep from doing this, use a
honing guide to hold your chisel as
you sharpen it. This simple device
clamps onto the blade. To adjust the
sharpening angle, move the guide
closer to or farther way from the cutting edge.

6-21 You can also purchase a
"rolling" honing guide to sharpen
gouges, skew chisels, and parting
tools. This device holds the gouge at
a constant angle but also allows you
to roll the blade from side to side as
you sharpen the bevel. Or, you can
rotate a skew chisel or a parting tool
until the bevel lies flat on the stone,
then lock it in position.

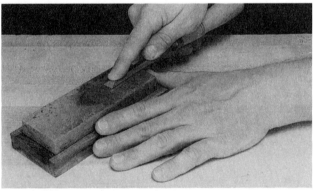

6-22 When you sharpen a chisel
for the first time, flatten the back.
Start with the coarsest stone and
grind the back perfectly flat. Then
work your way up through finer
abrasives to polish it. *However* (and
this is an important however), only
sharpen the *bevel* thereafter. Never
touch the back again except to polish
it. If you continue to grind away
metal from both the bevel and the
back every time you sharpen the
tool, the blade will become thinner
and weaker.

6-23 Use the coarsest stone to
remove the nicks from the tool and
reshape the cutting edge if it needs it.
Once you have the proper shape and
a crisp edge, work your way up
through progressively finer abrasives,
honing and polishing the surface of
the bevel. The finer you polish the
cutting edge, the sharper it becomes
and the better it will cut. Many experienced craftsmen polish their chisels
to a mirror finish.

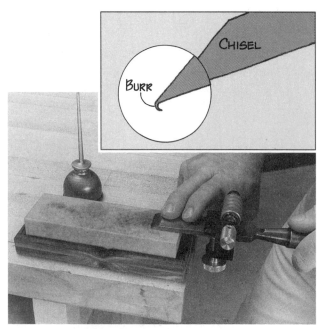

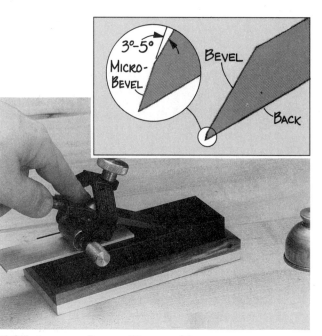

6-24 As you sharpen the bevel, a burr or *wire edge* will develop on the tip of the cutting edge. Ignore this until you've almost finished sharpening. Then turn the chisel over and rub the back against the last abrasive used. (Don't remove the honing guide yet.) To remove the last vestiges of this burr, it helps to take a few additional licks on the last stone, alternating between the bevel and the back. This is sometimes called *lapping the burr.*

6-25 Some craftsmen like to add a *microbevel* (also called a secondary bevel) to a cutting edge after they polish it. This tiny bevel, right at the point of the chisel, increases the bevel angle and makes the edge more durable. (It does *not,* by the way, make the edge sharper — that's a myth.) You probably don't need a microbevel for light- and medium-duty chisels, but if you frequently use hardwoods or do heavy work, it may help extend the time between sharpenings. To make a microbevel, adjust the honing guide or put a spacer under it to increase the sharpening angle by 3 to 5 degrees. Rub the cutting edge across the finest stone two or three times, no more.

TRY THIS TRICK

To put a mirror finish on a cutting edge, polish or *lap* it with microfine abrasive compounds such as jeweler's rouge or chromium oxide. The traditional tool for lapping is a leather strop glued to a hard, flat board. However, the leather may give slightly and round over the cutting edge. To prevent this, make a strop from a scrap of close-grained hardwood (such as maple or beech). Joint the wood surface flat and apply a polishing compound.

Sharpening a gouge requires a similar technique, but you must use special sharpening stones with convex surfaces such as *gouge slips* or *slipstones* to hone and polish the back. (*See Figure 6-26.*) Roll the bevel from side to side as you push the gouge back and forth on the sharpening stone. Remove the wire edge by alternately polishing the bevel and the back. Or, put a microbevel on the back. (*See Figure 6-27.*) This will also dispose of the wire edge.

To sharpen knives, you must grind, hone, and polish a bevel on *both* sides of the cutting edge so the angle between them is 15 to 20 degrees. Hold the knife blade 10 degrees or a little less from the surface of the stone, lock your wrist to maintain that angle, and wipe the blade across the stone. (*See Figure 6-28.*) Repeat for both sides, working your way up through progressively finer abrasives.

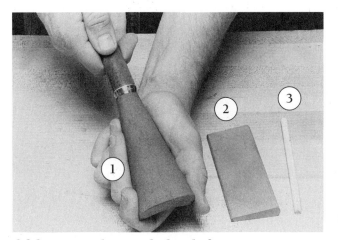

6-26 You can sharpen the bevel of a gouge with ordinary flat sharpening stones by rolling the bevel from side to side as you pass the blade back and forth. However, to hone and polish the concave back, you must use stones with a convex surface. The traditional choice is a tapered *gouge slip* (1), but you can also use the rounded edge of a *slipstone* (2) or a *round ceramic file* (3).

A Bit of Advice

Use a different set of stones to sharpen flat tools (such as chisels and plane irons) than you do to sharpen curved tools (such as knives and gouges). The curved cutting edges tend to dish out the stones, making it difficult to sharpen a straight edge.

6-27 If you wish to put a micro-bevel on a gouge, use a round ceramic file or a fine slipstone, tilt it at a 3- to 5-degree angle from the back, and *lightly* polish the back of the cutting edge for just a few seconds. This will also remove the wire edge.

6-28 The rules of thumb for sharpening a knife are the same as for a chisel — work your way from coarse to fine abrasives and maintain the sharpening angle as you do so. There are honing guides for knives, but they are expensive and it's hard to justify the cost for a tool used only occasionally. Instead, simply *lock your wrist* to keep the angle as you wipe the blade across the stone. Sharpen one side of the blade at a time, keeping your wrist locked as you move from stone to stone. This method is not as precise as a honing guide, but it's surprisingly accurate and produces a sharp edge.

STORAGE

Watch where you're laying chisels and gouges when you use them; if you accidentally rest them on another metal tool, you could damage the cutting edges. (*See Figure 6-29.*) Don't let them sit out when you're finished cutting; put them away. Hang them up or put them in a drawer near your workbench. (If you put them in a drawer, line the drawer bottom with felt or leather and put dividers between the chisels to keep them from banging into one another.)

Many craftsmen keep their chisels in a canvas *chisel roll*. This protects the tools when stored or carried from place to place.

To protect your chisels from rust, get rid of the closed-end tip protectors that come with many sets. These collect moisture on the cutting edges. Also, put a packet of *camphor* wherever you store your hand tools. (*See Figure 6-30.*)

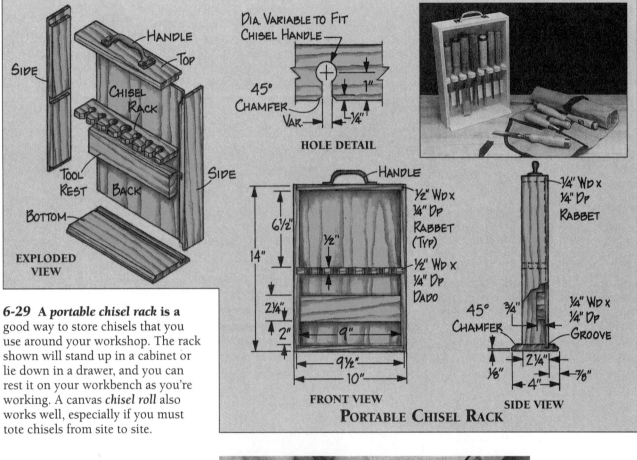

6-29 A portable chisel rack is a good way to store chisels that you use around your workshop. The rack shown will stand up in a cabinet or lie down in a drawer, and you can rest it on your workbench as you're working. A canvas *chisel roll* also works well, especially if you must tote chisels from site to site.

6-30 To protect your chisels, gouges, and other steel hand tools from rust, place a packet of *camphor* in the cabinet, drawer, or toolbox where you store them. With a knife, cut an X in the wrapper to expose the camphor to the air. It will evaporate slowly and condense on the metal surfaces nearby, coating them with a thin protective film. **Note:** You can purchase packets of camphor at most drug stores.

PUTTING A NEW HANDLE ON A CHISEL

No matter how well your chisels are made, eventually you'll have to fit them with new handles if you use them regularly. Some craftsmen recommend replacing the handles on *new* chisels, making a slightly different shape for each one to tell them apart easily. Whenever you decide to do this, you'll find it's an easy project.

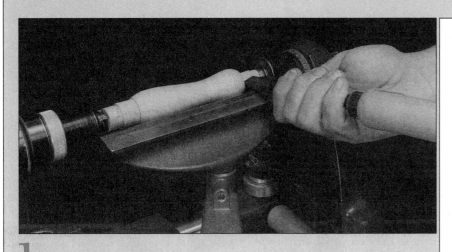

POSSIBLE DESIGNS FOR TANGED AND SOCKETED CHISEL HANDLES

1 **Turn the handle from a hard,** durable, close-grained wood such as beech, birch, hickory, or maple. Avoid open-grained woods such as oak; these tend to split easily and may also throw splinters. Use any design that fits your hand comfortably. You may want to choose from the six traditional handle patterns shown. You might also copy the existing handle or devise a personal design. A typical chisel handle should be about 6 inches long and 1¼ inches in diameter. Finish sand the handle on the lathe and apply several coats of a penetrating finish such as tung oil.

2 **To add a ferrule or a hoop** to your handle, cut metal rings from plumbing pipe. For each ring, turn a flat on the handle about ¹⁄₃₂ inch *larger* than the inside diameter of the ring. Heat the ring with a propane torch to expand it slightly, then force it onto the flat. As the ring cools, it will contract and tighten around the wood.

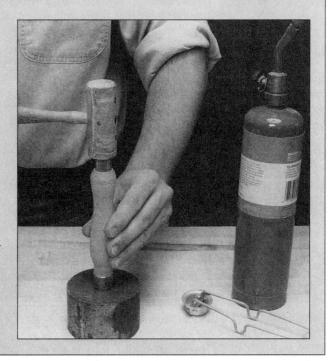

(continued) ▷

PUTTING A NEW HANDLE ON A CHISEL — CONTINUED

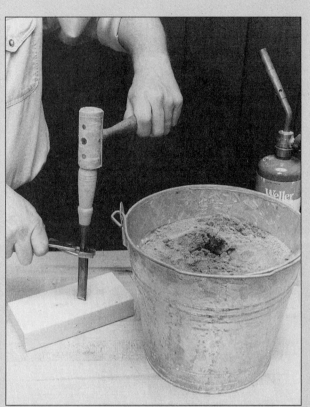

3 **To set a tanged chisel in a** new handle, first drill a starter hole in the front end of the handle. The diameter of the hole should be about the same as the width of the tang measured two-thirds of the way along its length, toward the neck; the depth should be ½ to ¾ inch shorter than the tang is long. Bury the blade of the chisel in a large can of sand and heat the tang with a propane torch. (The sand prevents the heat from traveling up the blade of the chisel and ruining the temper of the cutting edge.) Press the handle onto the tang, letting it burn away the wood inside the starter hole. Do this several times until the end of the handle is about ⅛ inch from the bolster. Place the nose of the chisel against a thick piece of soft wood and hit the handle with a mallet until the handle is seated against the bolster.

4 **The procedure is similar for** a socketed chisel. Turn a taper on the end of the handle to fit the socket as closely as possible. Bury the blade in sand and heat the socket with a torch. Press the tapered end of the handle into the socket, letting it burn away the wood. Then place the nose of the chisel against a thick piece of soft-wood and hit the handle a couple of good wallops with a mallet to seat it.

TOOL STEEL

To better understand how to choose, use, and care for hand tools, it helps to know something about the materials from which they are made. The cutting edges of hand tools — the blade of a chisel, the iron of a plane, and the bit of a drill — are all made from *tool steel,* a ferrous (iron-derived) metal specially prepared to take a sharp edge and retain it.

HOW TOOL STEEL IS MADE

Steel is essentially an alloy of iron and carbon. It begins as iron ore, which is refined to pig iron in a blast furnace. The pig iron is melted a second time in an atmosphere of pure oxygen to reduce *residual elements* (contaminants) such as silicon and manganese and to control the amount of carbon the metal contains. Ninety percent of the steel made is *tonnage steel* or *mild steel,* the stuff that bridges and car bodies are made from. This steel has a low carbon content (.10 to .30 percent) and is relatively soft and easy to work.

A small percentage of steel is made with a higher carbon content (.90 to 1.70 percent). The high carbon content allows the steel to be hardened, an important quality for cutting tools. This high-carbon steel may be melted a third time and small amounts of other elements — chromium, vanadium, tungsten, and molybdenum — added in varying proportions to make alloy steels with different working characteristics. These additives increase the ability of the steel to hold a cutting edge. Tungsten and vanadium, for example, make it possible to draw the steel out to an extremely sharp edge.

As it comes from the mill, the steel is not yet hard enough to make a good cutting tool. While it's in this soft state (metallurgists say the alloy steel is *annealed*), it's cut to size and forged (hammered) into a rough shape.

After forging, the steel is heated again, not hot enough to melt, only until its molecular structure changes into an extremely hard form. Then the steel is *quenched* (cooled quickly) to preserve this new structure. If it were allowed to cool slowly, it would revert to its original soft molecular composition.

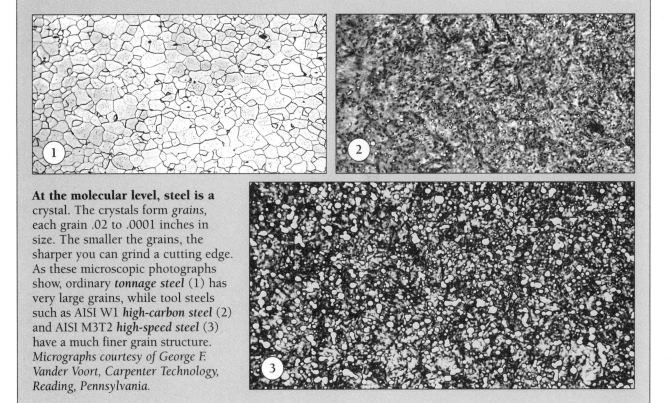

At the molecular level, steel is a crystal. The crystals form *grains,* each grain .02 to .0001 inches in size. The smaller the grains, the sharper you can grind a cutting edge. As these microscopic photographs show, ordinary *tonnage steel* (1) has very large grains, while tool steels such as AISI W1 *high-carbon steel* (2) and AISI M3T2 *high-speed steel* (3) have a much finer grain structure. *Micrographs courtesy of George F. Vander Voort, Carpenter Technology, Reading, Pennsylvania.*

(continued) ▷

TOOL STEEL — CONTINUED

The quenched steel is extremely hard — so hard that it's brittle and might shatter under use. So the steel is heated a final time to *temper* the metal and relieve some of its hardness, making it tougher. Cutting tools are normally tempered to between 58 and 61 on the Rockwell C-Scale of Hardness (abbreviated Rc). This makes them hard enough to take a fine cutting edge, but tough enough to withstand use. (To give you an idea of the hardness range, annealed steel is usually about Rc 20 and can be as hard as Rc 70 immediately after quenching.)

TYPES OF TOOL STEEL

There are many different types of tool steel, each with different properties, depending on the hardness and composition — the proportions of carbon and alloy elements in the metal. The American Iron and Steel Institute (AISI) labels these compositions for various applications. Here are a few examples:

■ Ordinary *high-carbon steel* (AISI 1055 to 1095), with no other alloys, is used for general toolmaking.

■ *W-type steels* (formulated to be quenched in water) retain a cutting edge better than most other types and are often used for chisels and plane irons.

■ *O-type steels* (formulated to be quenched in oil) are not as hard as the W-types and will not retain an edge quite as long, but they are easier to forge. These are used to make cutting tools that need a lot of shaping, such as gouges.

■ *D-type steels* (with high amounts of chromium) are best for knives and other tools with thin blades.

■ *S-type steels* (with high amounts of silicon and manganese) are shock-resistant. These make good cold chisels and other tools that must be struck repeatedly.

■ *M-type steels* (with high amounts of molybdenum) are sometimes referred to as high-speed steels (HSS). These retain their cutting edge even in the heat generated by the friction of high-speed operations. They are commonly used to make cutters for power tools — router bits, planer blades, shaper knives, drill bits, and so on.

■ *AISI 440C* is a variety of stainless (corrosion-resistant) steel that holds an edge almost as well as W-type steels and can be used for cutting tools that will be exposed to water or damp environments.

WHAT THIS MEANS TO YOU

The differences between types of steels are most apparent when the cutting edges are used continuously or run at high speeds. In hand tools, which are used intermittently at low speeds, these distinctions become very subtle — too subtle, in fact, for most woodworkers to detect or be concerned about. As long as the cutting edge is made of good quality tool steel and the type of steel is matched reasonably closely with the work to be done, the tool should perform well for you.

On the other hand, how the steel is tempered and the thickness of the cutter can make a noticeable difference. The harder the steel, the better it will hold a cutting edge. But hard steel becomes brittle, and cutting edges in particular are fragile — prone to chipping and breaking. When selecting chisels and other tools that are used to pry as well as to cut, it's best to stay away from extremely hard steels (above Rc 61).

In other tools, such as hand planes, you can get away with a cutting edge that's harder and more brittle by increasing the thickness of the cutter. This reinforces the brittle iron and helps prevent it from chattering, making the cutting edge less fragile and giving you a smoother cut. A few companies sell replacement irons for common hand planes that are slightly harder (Rc 62 to 63) and slightly thicker (about $3/32$ inch) than the irons that come with the planes. These improve the planes' performance — slightly.

By purchasing hand tools of reasonable quality from reputable manufacturers, you can be relatively assured of good, thick tool steel that is properly tempered. Don't be swayed by claims that the cutter is made from "high-carbon steel," "Sheffield steel," or the like. These are advertising gimmicks; they don't tell you anything about the quality, hardness, or thickness of the steel. "Laminated steel" is another subterfuge. This means that the manufacturer has wedded a small amount of hard, brittle tool steel to a lot of soft, cheap steel — a toolmaking technique that saves the manufacturer money, although you're usually asked to pay more for it.

7

STRIKING AND DRIVING

While most hand tools are pushed, pulled, or spun across a wooden surface, a few (such as chisels) are designed to be struck, driving the cutting edge into the wood. There is also a universe of fasteners that must be driven into the wood by striking — nails, brads, tacks, dowel pins, glaziers, sprigs, and ties. The tools designed to do all this striking and driving are hammers and mallets. Additionally, there is an important family of fasteners — wood screws — that are driven by turning them. There are several types of screwdrivers for doing this.

The origin of the hammer dates back to the beginnings of tool-making. Archaeologists have labeled the first primitive groups that produced stone tools as "anvil cultures." The two implements that they all had in common were holding devices (anvils) and striking devices (hammers.)

Screws and screwdrivers are a more recent development. Screw devices may have been used as early as 500 B.C., and in 285 A.D. the Greek scientist Pappus described the screw as one of the five basic "machines," along with the lever, pulley, wedge, and gear. But it was another 1,000 years before screws were commonly used as fasteners, and a few more centuries before the first slotted screws and screwdrivers appeared.

MALLETS AND HAMMERS

MALLETS

Mallets have two purposes. You can use them to drive chisels, gouges, and other tools with wooden handles, or you can use them to help assemble and disassemble wooden parts. In both cases, they are used to strike a wooden object. Because of this, mallet heads are often made from wood or a material slightly softer than wood.

There are four types of mallets commonly used in a woodworking shop:

■ A *carpenter's mallet* (sometimes called a joiner's mallet) has a square head and a hammer handle. It's a general-purpose design that can be used for many different tasks, depending on the size and weight of the mallet head. (*SEE FIGURE 7-1.*)

■ A *carver's mallet* has a round head and a round handle and is used for driving chisels and gouges. (*SEE FIGURE 7-2.*)

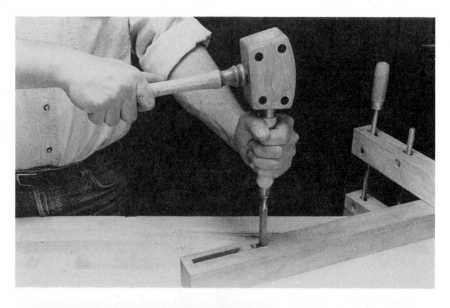

7-1 Carpenter's mallets are general-purpose striking tools with square heads. The handles usually have oval cross-sections, like hammer handles. These mallets come in different sizes and weights and can be used for many tasks, from driving chisels to assembling projects. Oftentimes, the striking surfaces are angled slightly down toward the butt end of the handle. This design lets you whack the end of a long chisel without having to hold the mallet at an uncomfortable angle.

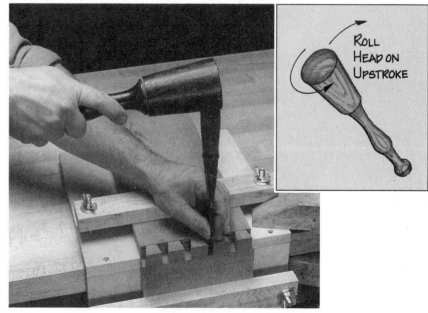

7-2 A carver's mallet has a cylindrical head and handle and is used to drive chisels and gouges. This head shape has three advantages. First, it makes the mallet easier to use. Because the entire head is a striking surface, you don't have to orient the mallet before you use it; just pick it up and swing. Second, the mallet head lasts longer — there is a much bigger striking surface to wear out. Finally, the mallet is easier on you. When you must use it for long periods, loosen your grip on the handle every time you swing back and rotate the mallet a fraction of a turn to hit the chisel with a different part of the head. Old-time craftsmen used this technique to relax their hands between strokes and reduce the strain on muscles and tendons.

ROLL HEAD ON UPSTROKE

■ A *dead-blow mallet* has a heavy head designed to distribute the force of each blow across the striking surface so that it doesn't mar the wood. This tool is often used for assembly and disassembly. (*See Figure 7-3.*)

■ A *rawhide mallet* has a head made from strips of leather rolled into a tight cylinder. This mallet is used for delicate operations. (*See Figure 7-4.*)

A Bit of Advice

When you must pound on your project with a mallet, put a scrap of soft wood over the surface. The scrap does the same thing as a dead-blow mallet — it distributes the force of the blow over a wider area and protects the surface. This is good practice, especially when using a mallet with a hard head.

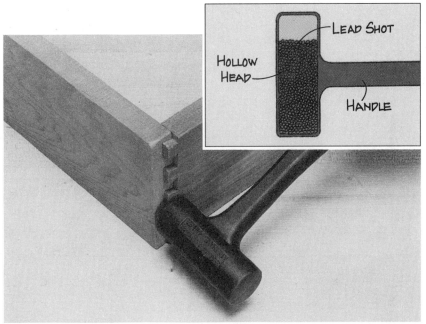

LEAD SHOT

HOLLOW HEAD

HANDLE

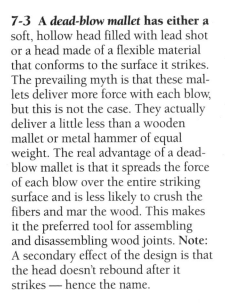

7-3 A *dead-blow mallet* has either a soft, hollow head filled with lead shot or a head made of a flexible material that conforms to the surface it strikes. The prevailing myth is that these mallets deliver more force with each blow, but this is not the case. They actually deliver a little less than a wooden mallet or metal hammer of equal weight. The real advantage of a dead-blow mallet is that it spreads the force of each blow over the entire striking surface and is less likely to crush the fibers and mar the wood. This makes it the preferred tool for assembling and disassembling wood joints. **Note:** A secondary effect of the design is that the head doesn't rebound after it strikes — hence the name.

7-4 The head of a *rawhide mallet* is made from rolled-up strips of leather which make the striking faces soft and resilient. These mallets tend to be small and light. Consequently, you can use them for delicate assemblies and other tasks where you want to deliver very light blows that won't mar the work or harm the tool. If you need to whack the end of a paring chisel or a small carving tool — which you shouldn't do, of course, but everyone does anyway — this is your best choice. **Note:** Like anything made from leather, a rawhide mallet becomes harder and more brittle with age and should be replaced when the head starts to crack. Unfortunately, you can't oil it to prolong its life; the oil would transfer to the wood.

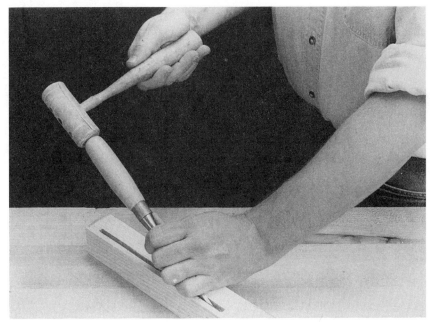

HAMMERS

At first, it may appear that the only difference between a mallet and a hammer is that a mallet head is made from wood or another soft material, while a hammer head is made of metal. But if you take a closer look, you'll find that a hammer is a more complex tool than a mallet.

The head of an ordinary *joiner's hammer*, the traditional type used by woodworkers, comes in several different weights, from 3½ to 12 ounces. It has a round striking surface or *face* about the size of a quarter. On the opposite side of the head, there is a tapered *cross pane* (or *cross peen*) with a narrow striking surface. Use the pane to start small nails and brads, then switch to the face to drive them. (*See Figures 7-5 and 7-6.*) **Note:** Although there were once many different designs for joiner's hammers, the Warrington pattern has eclipsed all the others in popularity. Today, joiner's hammers are frequently referred to as *Warrington hammers*.

The *tack hammer* was originally a small joiner's hammer, but the term has come to describe an upholsterer's hammer, a special tool for driving tacks with large, round heads. It, too, has a small face for starting the tacks and a larger one for driving them. (*See Figure 7-7.*)

A *claw hammer* has a "bifurcated" (split) pane, better known as a claw. This tool was invented by the Romans to pull nails as well as drive them. There are two types of claw hammers — a *ripping hammer* with a claw that comes straight out from the head, and a standard *claw hammer* with a curved claw. (*See Figure 7-8.*) The ripping hammer is used in remodeling and framing to pry structures apart, while the claw hammer is used for general construction and finish carpentry. Like joiner's hammers, the heads of claw hammers come in different weights, commonly ranging from 12 to 28 ounces.

Additionally, two related tools are used with hammers:

■ A *nail set* drives the heads of finish nails and brads flush with or below the wood surface. (*See Figure 7-9.*)

■ A *blind nail plane* lifts a sliver of wood so you can hide the head of a nail under it. (*See Figure 7-10.*)

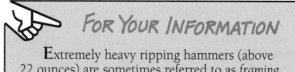

For Your Information

Extremely heavy ripping hammers (above 22 ounces) are sometimes referred to as *framing hammers* and are used to construct the frames of houses.

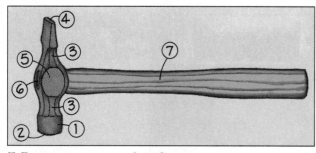

7-5 Many experienced craftsmen prefer a *joiner's hammer* (also called a cabinetmaker's hammer) for general woodworking tasks. This hammer has a steel head with a cylindrical *bell* (1) and a round striking *face* (2) on one side. The bell is attached to the head by a narrow *neck* (3). On the opposite side of the hammer is a tapered *cross pane* (4) with a narrow face. The flat sides or *cheeks* (5) should not be used for striking because there is a hole through the head at this point and the metal is thin. This hole or *eye* (6) slips over the end of the *handle* (7).

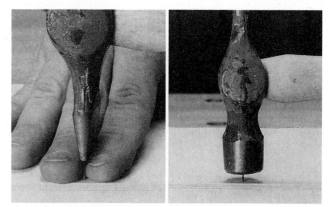

7-6 Use the pane of a joiner's hammer to start small nails and brads. The taper slips between your fingers without mashing them. Once the nail is started, turn the hammer around and drive the nail with the face. Joiner's hammers are available from 3½ to 12 ounces and can be used for a broad range of pounding tasks.

7-7 A *tack hammer* has two faces — a small, tapered face and a larger one. The smaller face is magnetized to hold a tack. When applying upholstery, you can't stretch the fabric over a frame, hold the tack, and swing the hammer all at once; you'd need three hands. Instead, just stick the tack head to the hammer and strike the surface wherever you want to place the tack. Once the tack is started, turn the hammer around and finish driving it with the larger face.

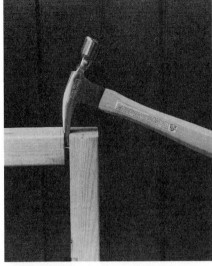

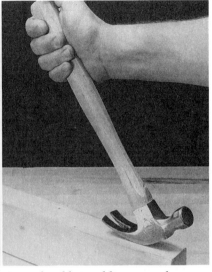

7-8 A *ripping hammer* (left) has a straight pane or claw that comes out straight from the head. This is handy for remodeling jobs — you can use it to remove old siding, moldings, clapboards, and so on. A regular *claw hammer* (right) has a curved claw to provide additional leverage when pulling nails. These are used for general woodworking, carpentry, and finish carpentry. Both types of hammers are commonly available in weights between 12 and 28 ounces.

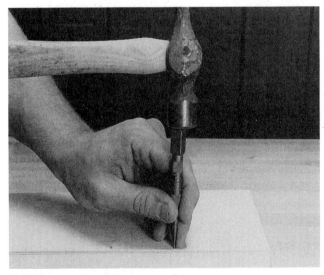

7-9 Don't use a hammer to drive a finish nail flush with the surface. Instead, stop when the head of the nail is a fraction of an inch *above* the surface. Then, continue driving it with a *nail set,* as shown, to keep the face of the hammer from marring the wood surface. If you wish, set the nail — that is, drive the head slightly *below* the surface. Then you can cover the head with wood putty or stick shellac to make it less noticeable.

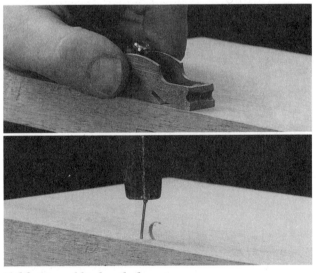

7-10 Use a *blind nail plane* to completely hide the head of a finish nail. Raise a tiny sliver of wood with the plane and drive the nail into the recess left by the sliver. Set the head of the nail below the surface of the recess, then glue the sliver back in place, using a piece of masking tape to hold it while the glue dries. After you remove the tape and sand the surface, you won't be able to tell where the nail is.

SCREWDRIVERS

TIPS, SHAFTS, AND HANDLES

Screwdrivers are classified according to their *tip* and the type of screw they are designed to drive. There are many different screws, but only a handful are commonly used in woodworking. Consequently, you only need to keep a few types of screwdrivers in your toolbox (*SEE FIGURE 7-11*):

■ A *blade screwdriver* drives slotted screws — screws with a single groove in the head. The tips come in eight widths from 3/32 to 1/2 inch to accommodate different sizes of screws.

■ A *Phillips screwdriver* has a pointed, cross-shaped tip to drive Phillips screws with cross-shaped recesses in their heads. The tips come in five sizes from #0 to #4 for different screws.

■ A *square-drive screwdriver* (also called a Robertson screwdriver) has a square tip to drive screws with square recesses in their heads. The tips come in four sizes from #0 to #3. Square-drive screws are not yet common in hardware stores; they are available mostly through mail-order suppliers. However, they have become popular with some woodworkers because there is less chance that the screwdriver will slip and strip the heads.

You have many more choices in handle and shaft patterns. Few of the handle designs affect the utility or the purpose of the tool; most are simply aesthetic. The same holds true for the shafts of Phillips and square-drive screwdrivers. However, the shafts of most blade screwdrivers end in a wedge shape. These ream out counterbores as you drive screws below the wood surface, and they are more likely to slip and mar the wood. Only the *cabinet* pattern has a straight shaft and a hollow-ground blade to prevent these problems. (*SEE FIGURES 7-12 AND 7-13.*)

There are also some special designs. An *offset screwdriver* has a bent shaft to help you drive screws in restricted spaces. (*SEE FIGURE 7-14.*) Screwdrivers with interchangeable tips do the work of several tools. (*SEE FIGURE 7-15.*)

7-11 Three types of screws are commonly used in woodworking, and three types of screwdrivers are needed to drive them. Use a flat or *blade screwdriver* (1) with slotted screws (1a), a *Phillips screwdriver* (2) with Phillips screws (2a), and a *square-drive screwdriver* (3) with square-drive screws (3a). The tips of each type of screwdriver come in several sizes.

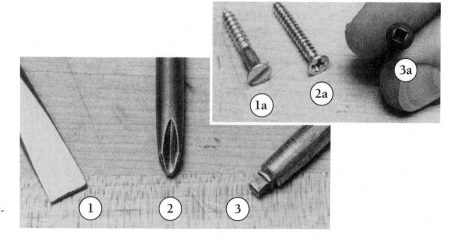

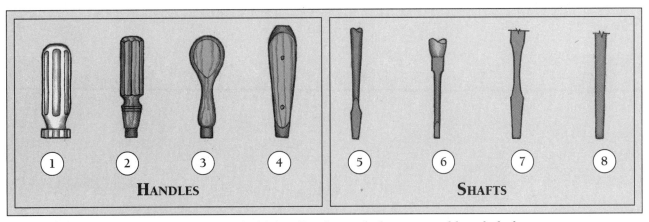

HANDLES   **SHAFTS**

7-12 When purchasing screw-drivers, you have a choice of handle and shaft patterns. The four most common handles are the round or **barrel** (1), the octagonal **box** (2), the **egg** or **oval** (3), and the two-piece *scale* (4) handle. There is little variety in the shafts of Phillips and square-drive screwdrivers, but there are four types of blade screwdriver shafts to consider — *utility* (5), *cabinet* (6), *London* (7), and *Scotch* (8), although the last two patterns are becoming scarce. Additionally, shafts come in many different lengths, from 1½ to 12 inches long.

7-13 When selecting blade screw-drivers specifically for woodworking, look for *cabinet* pattern shafts. The tapered, wedge-shaped ends on utility shafts and other designs do not work as well when driving slotted screws. Because the tip is not ground square, the blade tends to ride up and out of the slot as you turn it. This, in turn, causes the screwdriver to slip and possibly mar the wood surface. And if you drive a screw below the surface, the wedge shape will ream out the counterbore and the screw plugs will no longer fit.

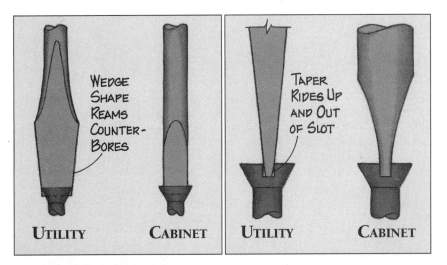

7-14 An *offset screwdriver* has no handle, just a shank with tips at both ends. The shank is bent in the shape of a crank. This design lets you drive screws in restricted areas.

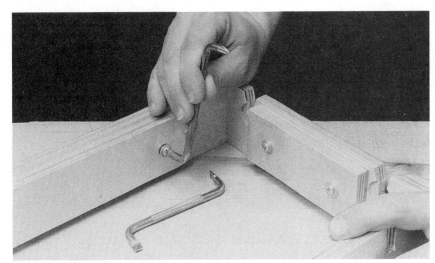

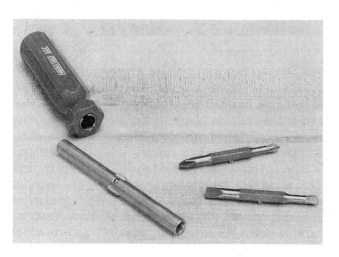

7-15 A screwdriver with inter-changeable bits can be handy if you must drive several types of screws. Some of these tools have a hollow "magazine" handle to hold a selection of tips. The screwdriver shown has a reversible shaft and reversible tips, letting you drive two different sizes of both slotted screws and Phillips screws.

Mechanical screwdrivers employ some device to help turn the screwdriver so you don't have to do as much work. A *ratchet screwdriver* has a ratchet in the handle so the shaft only turns in one direction. A *Yankee screwdriver* has a spiral ratchet drive, similar to a push drill. (*SEE FIGURE 7-16.*)

TRY THIS TRICK

If you find it difficult to drive screws through a hard material, rub the threads with paraffin or paste wax. This lubricates the screws so there is less resistance when you turn them.

SHARPENING SCREWDRIVERS

The tips of cabinet-pattern blade screwdrivers have crisp, square edges. These eventually become dull, and as they do, the tips begin to slip in the screw slots. To resharpen the tips, hollow-grind the faces. They should fit the screw slots fairly close; there should be very little play.

TRY THIS TRICK

You can easily regrind a utility screwdriver to a cabinet pattern. File the edges of the wedge-shaped end straight, parallel with the shaft. Then hollow-grind the tapered blade.

7-16 A *ratchet screwdriver* (1) has a ratchet handle that can be set to turn the shaft only clockwise, only counterclockwise, or both directions, whichever you need at the moment. A *Yankee screwdriver* (2) does the same, but it has a spiral ratchet drive that turns the shaft as you push down on the handle. Both mechanical screwdrivers let you drive screws in or out without ever having to remove the tip from the screw head.

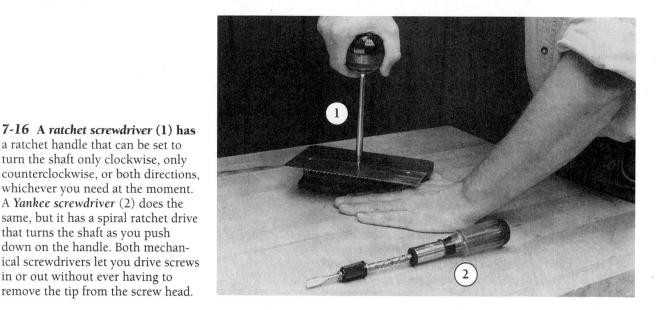

PROJECTS

8

MAKING HAND TOOLS

Once, every woodworker made his own tools. Before the mid-nineteenth century, a craftsman learned a woodworking trade while he was apprenticed to a master, and he built his first set of tools with the master's guidance. Thereafter, he made tools as he needed them, designing them to fit the tasks he had to do and buying steel blades and other metal parts from a local blacksmith.

Today, few of us have the time or the resources to make many of our own woodworking tools. Most implements have become too sophisticated to craft in a home workshop. However, there are still a few hand tools that you can make easily using metal and plastic parts from your local hardware store or a mail-order supplier.

Sometimes, you can make them better than what you could buy. This chapter offers a few examples.

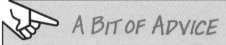

A BIT OF ADVICE

For durability, hand tools should be made from extremely hard, closed-grain woods. Often, craftsmen use tropical woods (referred to as *exotics*) such as rosewood, coco-bolo, bubinga, and others with the desired characteristics. If you work with tropical woods, purchase them from a responsible supplier who respects the sensitive environments of the rain forests from which they come. For a list of these suppliers, ask for the "Good Wood" list from:

Woodworker's Alliance for Rainforest Protection
Box 133
Coos Bay, OR 97420

If you would rather work with domestic hardwoods, maple, birch, and beech are also good choices.

SHOULDER AND ROUTER PLANES

A *shoulder plane* and a *router plane* are invaluable aids when fitting joints and installing hardware. A shoulder plane trims edges, rabbets, and tenons; a router plane cleans the bottoms of dadoes, grooves, and mortises.

On the shoulder plane shown below, the plane iron is bedded in a wooden body and held in place by a wedge. A T-knob advances the blade to set the depth of cut precisely. On the router plane, the handle is sculpted from wood, but the base is clear plastic, giving you better visibility than commercially made models. Both planes use irons available from mail-order companies.

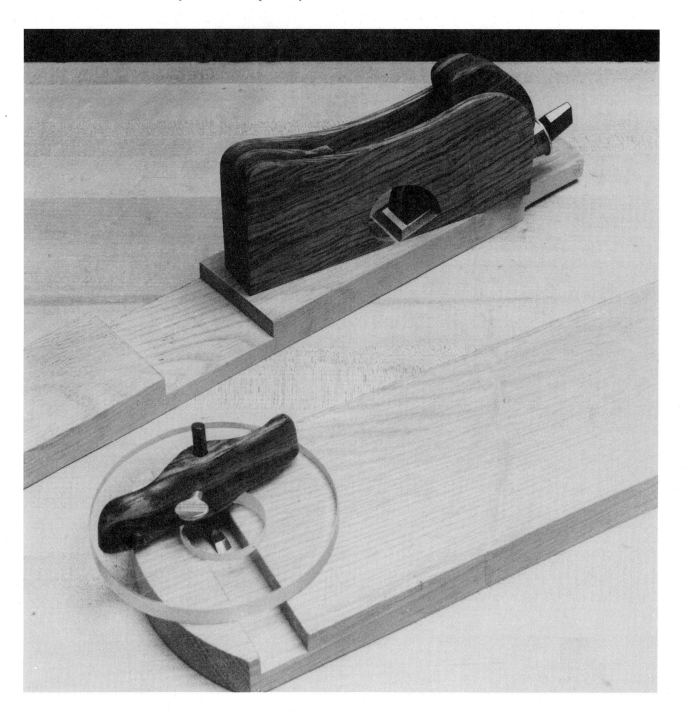

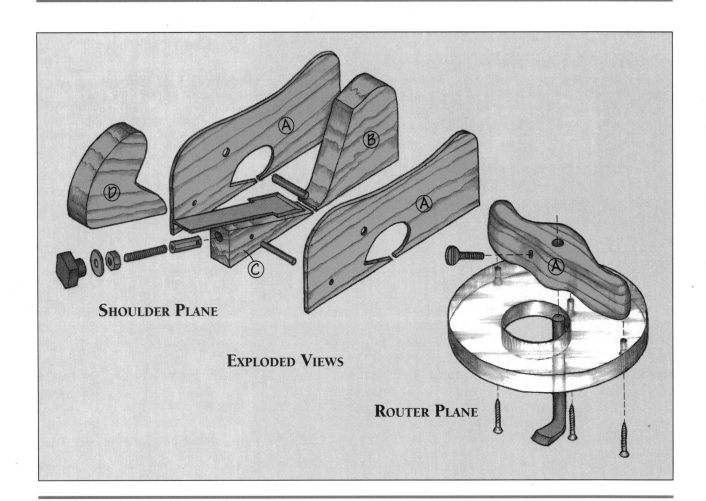

SHOULDER PLANE

EXPLODED VIEWS

ROUTER PLANE

MATERIALS LIST (FINISHED DIMENSIONS)

Parts

Shoulder Plane

A.	Sides (2)	$\frac{3}{16}''$ x $2\frac{3}{4}''$ x 7"
B.	Nose	$\frac{3}{4}''$ x $2\frac{3}{4}''$ x $3\frac{3}{8}''$
C.	Heel	$\frac{3}{4}''$ x $1\frac{1}{4}''$ x $3\frac{1}{2}''$
D.	Wedge	$\frac{3}{4}''$ x $2\frac{5}{8}''$ x $3\frac{1}{2}''$

Router Plane

A.	Handle	1" x 1" x $3\frac{7}{8}''$

Hardware

Shoulder Plane

Plane iron for Record Improved Bullnose Plane or tool steel blank ($\frac{1}{8}''$ x $1\frac{1}{8}''$ x 4")

$\frac{1}{4}''$-20 T-knob (with threaded insert)

$\frac{1}{4}''$-20 x $1\frac{3}{4}''$ Threaded rod

$\frac{1}{4}''$ x 1" Fender washer

$\frac{1}{4}''$-20 Jamb nut

$\frac{1}{4}''$-20 Coupling nut

$\frac{1}{4}''$ x $1\frac{1}{8}''$ Steel pin

$\frac{1}{8}''$ x $1\frac{1}{8}''$ Steel pin

Router Plane

$\frac{3}{8}''$ Clear acrylic plastic disk (4" diameter)

#8 x $\frac{3}{4}''$ Brass flathead wood screws (3)

#10-24 x $\frac{1}{2}''$ Thumbscrew plane iron for Stanley #271 Router Plane

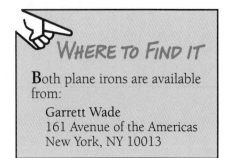

WHERE TO FIND IT

Both plane irons are available from:

Garrett Wade
161 Avenue of the Americas
New York, NY 10013

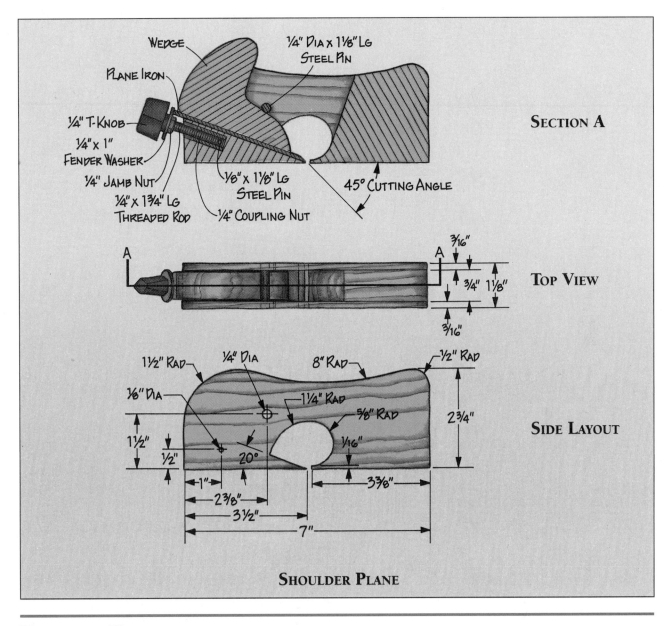

SHOULDER PLANE

Section A labels:
- WEDGE
- PLANE IRON
- ¼" T-KNOB
- ¼" x 1" FENDER WASHER
- ¼" JAMB NUT
- ¼" x 1¾" LG THREADED ROD
- ¼" DIA x 1⅛" LG STEEL PIN
- ⅛" x 1⅛" LG STEEL PIN
- ¼" COUPLING NUT
- 45° CUTTING ANGLE

SECTION A

Top View labels: 3/16", 3/4", 1⅛", 3/16", A

TOP VIEW

Side Layout labels: 1½" RAD, ¼" DIA, 8" RAD, ½" RAD, ⅛" DIA, 1¼" RAD, ⅝" RAD, 2¾", 1½", ½", 20°, 1/16", 1", 2⅜", 3½", 3⅜", 7"

SIDE LAYOUT

PLAN OF PROCEDURE

MAKING THE SHOULDER PLANE

1 Cut the parts to size and shape. Select a hard, closed-grain wood and cut the parts to the sizes given in the Materials List. Stack the sides face to face and stick them together with double-faced carpet tape. Lay out the patterns on the sides, nose, heel, and wedge, as shown in the *Side Layout, Nose Layout, Heel Layout,* and *Wedge Layout.*

Cut the profiles of the parts with a band saw, scroll saw, or coping saw. For accuracy, cut wide of the layout line, then file up to it. Sand the sawed edges of the wedge and those edges on the nose and heel that will be *inside* the assembled plane. (Don't bother to sand the outside edges yet.)

2 Drill holes in the heel and sides. With the sides still stacked, drill a ¼-inch-diameter hole through them to hold the steel pin. Take the stack apart and discard the tape. Also drill a ¹³⁄₃₂-inch-diameter, 1³⁄₁₆-inch-deep hole in the back edge of the heel, as shown in the *Heel Layout/End View.* Note that this hole must be parallel with the surface that supports the plane iron.

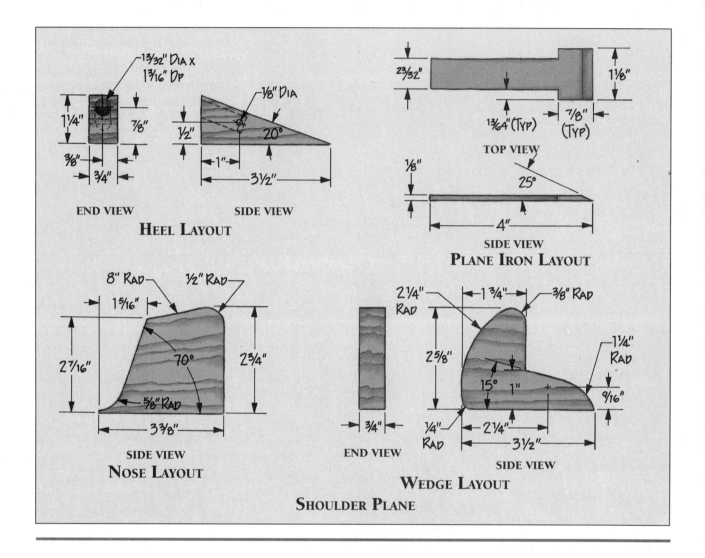

HEEL LAYOUT

END VIEW   SIDE VIEW

PLANE IRON LAYOUT

TOP VIEW

SIDE VIEW

NOSE LAYOUT

SIDE VIEW

WEDGE LAYOUT

END VIEW   SIDE VIEW

SHOULDER PLANE

3 Assemble the wooden parts. Fasten the side, nose, and heel together with wood glue, making sure that there's a ⅛-inch-wide gap between the nose and the heel to create the mouth of the plane. Insert the ¼-inch-diameter steel pin in the holes in the sides to help align them.

After the glue dries, secure the pin to the sides with epoxy cement. Sand the outside surfaces and joint the

TRY THIS TRICK

To keep the parts of the shoulder plane from sliding around when you glue them up, sprinkle a little sanding grit on the wood after you spread the glue. To do this, rub two pieces of 100-grit sandpaper together above the glue-covered surfaces. Don't overdo it; you just need a few grains of abrasive on each surface.

A SAFETY REMINDER

Because the plane is too short to joint safely, attach it to an 18-inch long scrap with double-faced carpet tape, aligning both bottom surfaces flush. Pass both the scrap and the plane across the jointer, holding the scrap against the fence.

sole square to the sides. The sole must be precisely 90 degrees from the side for the plane to operate properly.

4 Secure the coupling nut. Press the coupling nut into the stopped hole in the back of the heel. Drill a ⅛-inch-diameter hole through the plane and the nut. As you drill, clear the metal shavings from the bit often to prevent them from enlarging the ⅛-inch-diameter hole in the wooden side. Then drive a steel pin through the hole to lock the coupling nut in place. If the pin seems loose, hold it in place with epoxy cement.

5 **Grind and sharpen the plane iron**. If you have decided to make your own plane iron, grind the blank to the T-shape shown in the *Plane Iron Layout*. Then grind a 25-degree bevel on the cutting edge and sharpen it.

6 **Finish the plane.** Screw the threaded rod into the T-knob. Slide the fender washer onto the rod and lock the parts together with the jamb nut. Insert the plane iron in the mouth of the plane. Sand the face of

the wedge until it slides easily between the sides, then lock the iron in place with the wedge. Screw the knob assembly in the coupling nut until the washer pushes against the plane iron. Turn the knob, slowly advancing the iron until you can make a paper-thin cut with the plane.

When you're satisfied that the plane is working correctly, remove the wedge, the plane iron, and the knob assembly. Finish sand the wooden surfaces (except for the sole) and apply a penetrating finish such as tung oil or Danish oil. Let the finish dry, then wax and buff the surfaces. Reassemble the plane and adjust the plane iron.

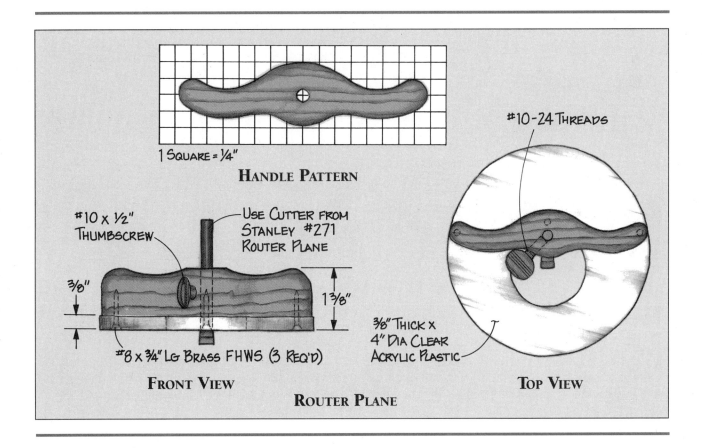

1 SQUARE = ¼"

HANDLE PATTERN

#10 × ½" THUMBSCREW

USE CUTTER FROM STANLEY #271 ROUTER PLANE

#10-24 THREADS

3/8"

1 3/8"

#8 × ¾" LG BRASS FHWS (3 REQ'D)

3/8" THICK × 4" DIA CLEAR ACRYLIC PLASTIC

FRONT VIEW

TOP VIEW

ROUTER PLANE

MAKING THE ROUTER PLANE

1 **Cut and drill the sole.** Lay out the sole on a ⅜-inch-thick sheet of clear acrylic plastic, as shown in the *Sole Layout*. Cut the disk and bore a 1⅜-inch-diameter hole through the interior. (Note that this hole is offset from the center.) Drill and countersink ⁵⁄₆₄-inch-diameter pilot holes for the screws that will hold the handle to the sole.

2 **Cut the handle to size and lay out the shape.** Select a hard, closed-grain wood and cut it to the size specified for the handle in the *Materials List*. Lay out the profile of the handle as shown in the *Handle Pattern*. Use the sole as a template to mark the location of the ⁵⁄₆₄-inch-diameter pilot holes.

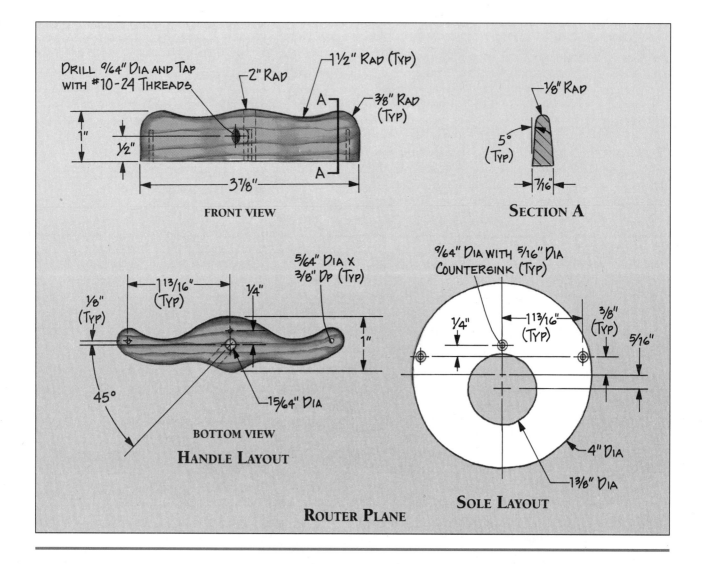

Drill ⁹⁄₆₄" Dia and Tap with #10-24 Threads

2" Rad

1½" Rad (Typ)

⅜" Rad (Typ)

A

A

1"

½"

3⅞"

FRONT VIEW

⅛" Rad

5° (Typ)

⁷⁄₁₆"

SECTION A

1¹³⁄₁₆" (Typ)

¼"

5⁄₆₄" Dia x ⅜" Dp (Typ)

⅛" (Typ)

1"

45°

15⁄₆₄" Dia

BOTTOM VIEW

HANDLE LAYOUT

9⁄₆₄" Dia with 5⁄₁₆" Dia Countersink (Typ)

¼"

1¹³⁄₁₆" (Typ)

⅜" (Typ)

5⁄₁₆"

4" Dia

1⅜" Dia

SOLE LAYOUT

ROUTER PLANE

3 Drill the holes in the handle stock and cut it to shape. Drill a ¹⁵⁄₆₄-inch-diameter hole through the center of the handle to hold the plane iron. Then bore a ⁹⁄₆₄-inch-diameter hole through the side of the handle, intersecting the first hole, as shown in the *Handle Layout/Bottom View.* Cut threads in this hole with a #10-24 tap. Also drill three ⁵⁄₆₄-inch-diameter pilot holes in the bottom of the handle. After drilling the holes, cut the handle profile.

4 Shape the handle. Using a cabinetmaker's rasp and a file, taper the handle as shown in *Section A,* then round over the top edges as shown in the *Handle Layout/Front View.*

5 Assemble and finish the router plane. Attach the handle to the sole with flathead wood screws. (The heads of these wood screws must rest slightly below the surface of the sole.) Turn a #10 thumbscrew into the threaded hole in the side of the handle. Insert the plane iron in the handle and lock it in place with the thumbscrew. **Note:** As long as the handle is made from a sufficiently hard wood, the threads will not strip out with normal use.

When you're satisfied the router plane works properly, remove the plane iron, thumbscrew, and sole from the handle. Finish sand the handle and apply a penetrating finish. Let the finish dry, then wax and buff the handle. Reassemble the plane and adjust the plane iron.

USING THE ROUTER PLANE

The router plane reaches down into a groove, dado, or mortise to shave the bottom. To do this, the iron extends far beneath the sole — much farther than on other planes. Because of this, the router plane requires a different technique to use it.

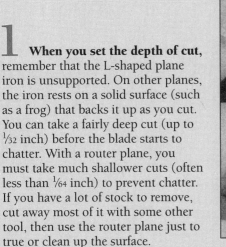

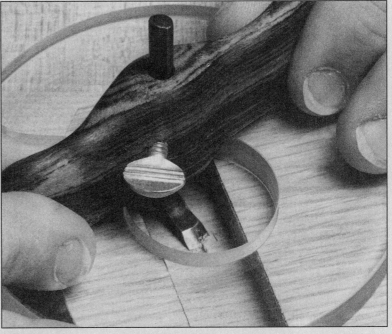

1 **When you set the depth of cut,** remember that the L-shaped plane iron is unsupported. On other planes, the iron rests on a solid surface (such as a frog) that backs it up as you cut. You can take a fairly deep cut (up to $\frac{1}{32}$ inch) before the blade starts to chatter. With a router plane, you must take much shallower cuts (often less than $\frac{1}{64}$ inch) to prevent chatter. If you have a lot of stock to remove, cut away most of it with some other tool, then use the router plane just to true or clean up the surface.

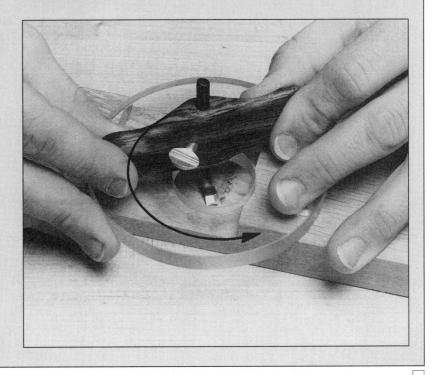

2 **It's often easier to cut wide** surfaces with a router plane if you *don't* move it in a straight line. Instead, *pivot* the plane in short arcs. Hold one side of the handle stationary and swing the other side partway around it.

BEADING TOOL

A *beading tool* scrapes a delicate shape near the edge of a workpiece. It offers two advantages over routers and shapers: It's less likely to chip or tear figured wood grain, and if you need a special shape, you'll find it much easier to grind a scraper blade than to create a new router bit or shaper cutter.

This beader has a wooden body and handles, cut from a single block of wood. It mounts commercially available blades, or you can make your own from an old hand scraper.

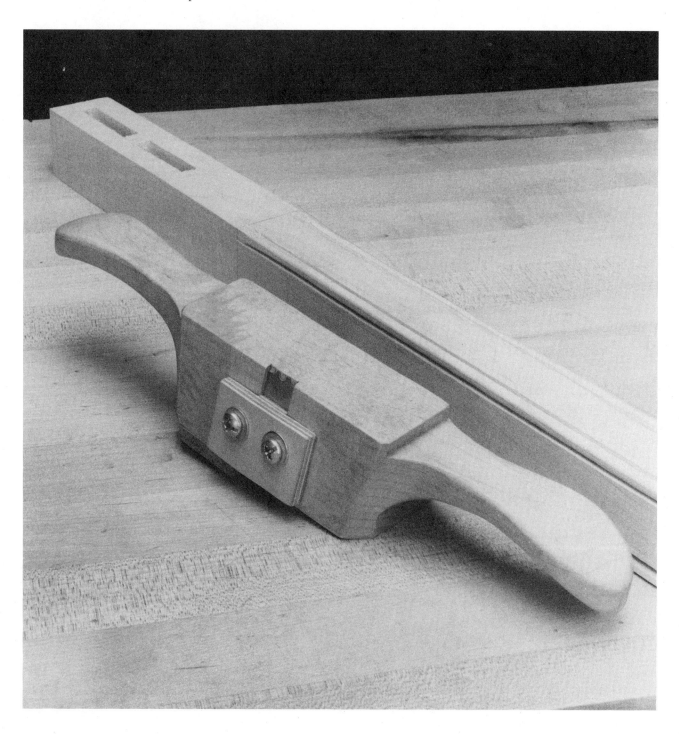

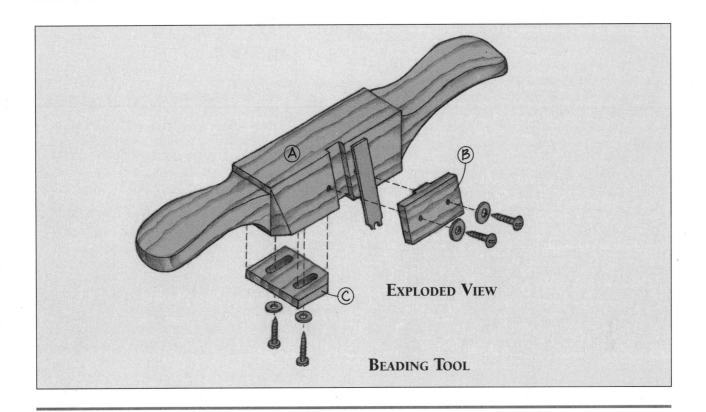

EXPLODED VIEW

BEADING TOOL

MATERIALS LIST (FINISHED DIMENSIONS)

Parts

A. Body   1⅞" x 2" x 12¾"
B. Clamp   ⅜" x 1¼" x 2"
C. Fence   ¼" x 1¾" x 2"

Hardware

#10 x 1" Panhead screws (2)
#8 x ¾" Roundhead wood screws
  (2)
#10 Flat washers (2)
#8 Flat washers (2)
Scraper blade (1/16" x ⅝" x 2")

WHERE TO FIND IT

You can purchase ⅝-inch-wide "scratch stock" blanks to make scraper blades from:

Garrett Wade
161 Avenue of the Americas
New York, NY 10013

Or you can purchase ready-made ⅝-inch-wide scraper blades from:

Lie-Nielsen Toolworks, Inc.
Route 1
Warren, ME 04864

PLAN OF PROCEDURE

1 Cut the parts to size. Select a hard, closed-grain wood, and cut the body to the size given in the Materials List. Cut the clamp several inches wider than specified, and cut the fence several inches longer — this will make them easier and safer to machine. **Note:** Instead of cutting the fence and clamp stock oversize, you can attach these small parts to a larger scrap with double-faced carpet tape. This, too, will help you to machine them.

2 Drill holes in the body and the clamp. Rip a 10-degree bevel in one edge of the body, as shown in the *End View*. Lay out the side pattern, as shown in the *Body Pattern/Side View,* on the beveled edge. Also lay out the slots and holes on the body, as shown in the *Front Detail* and *Bottom Detail.* Drill %4-inch-diameter, ⅝-inch-deep pilot holes in the beveled edge (perpendicular to the bevel) and 5⁄64-inch-diameter, ½-inch-deep pilot holes in the bottom face. Then

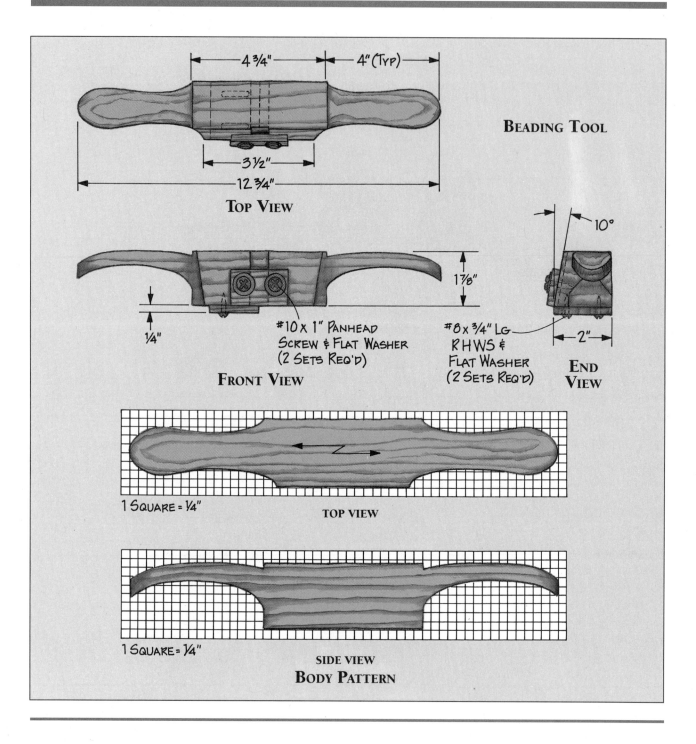

BEADING TOOL

4 3/4" — 4" (TYP)

3 1/2"

12 3/4"

TOP VIEW

10°

1 7/8"

1/4"

#10 x 1" PANHEAD
SCREW & FLAT WASHER
(2 SETS REQ'D)

FRONT VIEW

#8 x 3/4" LG
RHWS &
FLAT WASHER
(2 SETS REQ'D)

2"

**END
VIEW**

1 SQUARE = 1/4"   **TOP VIEW**

1 SQUARE = 1/4"   **SIDE VIEW**
BODY PATTERN

drill ³/₁₆-inch-diameter holes through the clamp, as shown in the *Clamp Layout/Back View.*

3 Cut the joinery in the body, clamp, and fence. Using a table-mounted router or a dado cutter, cut a ⅝-inch-wide, ¼-inch-deep dado in the bottom face of the body for chip clearance and a ⅝-inch-wide, ⅛-inch-deep dado in the beveled edge to hold the

scraper blades. Also make an ¹¹/₁₆-inch-wide, ⅛-inch-deep rabbet in each end of the clamp stock, as shown in the *Clamp Layout/Top View,* and ³/₁₆-inch-wide slots in the fence stock, as shown in the *Fence Layout.* Then chamfer one corner of the fence stock. After cutting all the joinery in the clamp and fence stock, cut the parts to size.

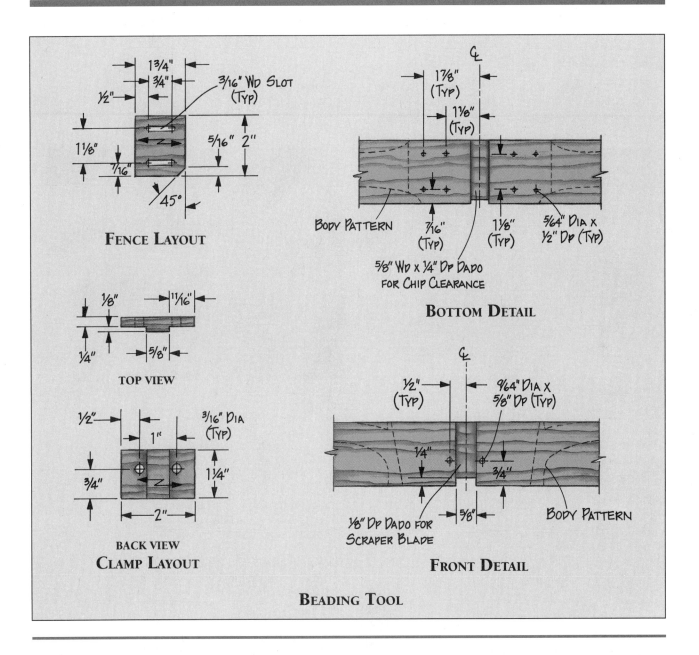

FENCE LAYOUT

TOP VIEW

BACK VIEW
CLAMP LAYOUT

BOTTOM DETAIL

FRONT DETAIL

BEADING TOOL

4 Cut the shape of the body. Create the shape of the body by making a compound cut with a band saw. Cut the side pattern first (with the stock resting on the edge that's *not* beveled), carefully saving the waste. Fasten the waste back to the block with masking tape and lay out the top pattern, as shown in the *Body Pattern/Top View,* on the top face. Cut the top pattern (with the stock resting on the bottom face), then discard the waste and the tape. The body should have two long, curved handles protruding from the ends. Sand the sawed surfaces and round over the hard edges of the handles with a rasp and file to make them comfortable to grasp.

5 Assemble and finish the beader. Fasten the fence to the bottom of the body with #8 roundhead wood screws and washers. Note that you can mount the fence in four different positions, two on each side of the chip clearance dado. Rest a scraper blade in the dado in the beveled edge and place the clamp over it. Secure the clamp and the blade to the body with #10 panhead screws and washers.

When you're satisfied the parts of the beader fit together properly, remove the scraper blade, clamp, and fence from the body. Finish sand the wooden parts and apply a penetrating finish. Let the finish dry, then wax and buff the surfaces. Reassemble the beader.

USING THE BEADING TOOL

Scraping a shape with a beading tool is, in many ways, much easier than using a molding plane or some other cutting tool. However, because the beading tool removes less stock with each pass, it takes much longer.

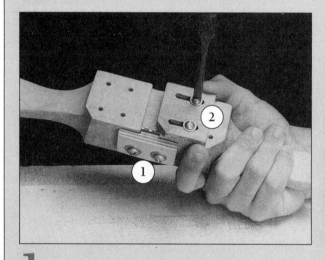

1 **To adjust the depth of cut on** a beading tool, loosen the clamp screws (1) and slide the scraper blade up or down. To adjust the fence position, move the fence to the mounting position that will work best for the particular job you have to do. To fine-tune the position, leave the fence screws (2) loose and slide the fence from side to side. Then tighten all screws.

2 **To use the beading tool,** grasp it in both hands. Hold the fence against the edge of the stock and draw the tool along it, pressing down *lightly*. The scraper blade will scratch away a little stock as it begins to scrape the shape. Repeat as many times as needed, making each pass in a long, fluid movement. When the sole of the beading tool rests flat on the wood surface and the scraper blade no longer removes any stock, the shape is complete.

3 **To create your own blades** for the beading tool, lay out a *negative* of the shape you wish to cut on the end of a ⅝-inch-wide tool steel blank. If you can, grind away most of the metal waste with a grinding wheel. Then file the shape up to the layout line with needle files.

CARPENTER'S AND CARVER'S MALLETS

A *carpenter's mallet* offers two flat wooden faces for general pounding operations. A *carver's mallet* has a cylindrical face designed for driving chisels and gouges. Both are simple turning projects.

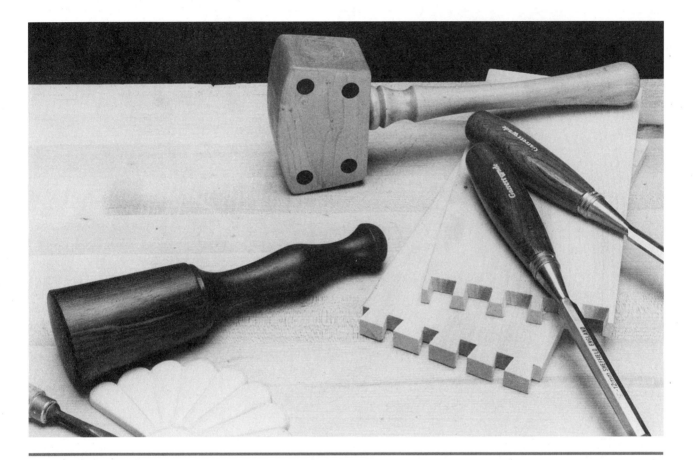

MATERIALS LIST
(FINISHED DIMENSIONS)

Parts

Carpenter's Mallet

A.	Head	2" x 2¾" x 4½"
B.	Handle	1⅜" dia. x 12"
C.	Wedge	⅛" x ¾" x 1"
D.	Reinforcing dowels (4)	½" dia. x 2"

Carver's Mallet

A.	Mallet	2½" dia. x 9¼"

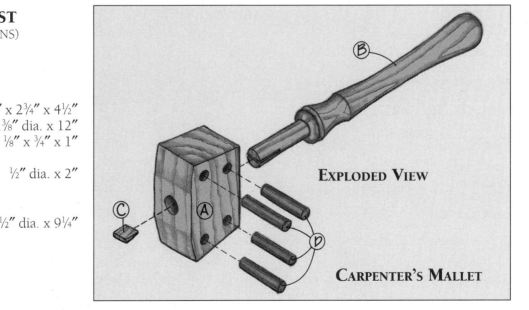

EXPLODED VIEW

CARPENTER'S MALLET

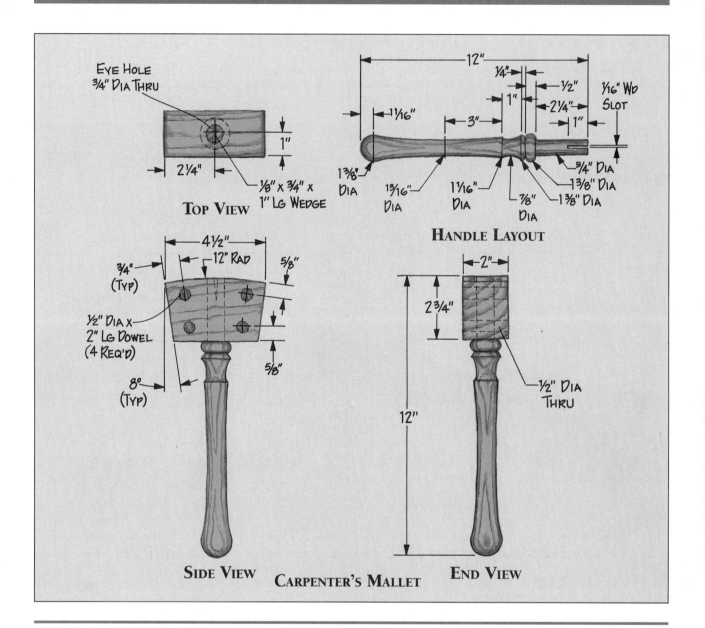

EYE HOLE
¾" DIA THRU

1"

2¼"

⅛" x ¾" x
1" LG WEDGE

TOP VIEW

12"

¼"
½"
1"
2¼"
1"
1⁄16" WD
SLOT

1 1⁄16"

3"

1⅜"
DIA

13⁄16"
DIA

1 1⁄16"
DIA

⅞"
DIA

¾" DIA
1⅜" DIA
1⅜" DIA

HANDLE LAYOUT

4½"
12" RAD
5⁄8"

¾"
(TYP)

½" DIA X
2" LG DOWEL
(4 REQ'D)

8°
(TYP)

5⁄8"

2"

2¾"

12"

½" DIA
THRU

SIDE VIEW   **CARPENTER'S MALLET**   **END VIEW**

PLAN OF PROCEDURE

MAKING THE CARPENTER'S MALLET

1 **Cut the stock to size.** Select a hard, closed-grain wood and cut the head to the size given in the Materials List. Cut the handle stock about 1½ inches square and 14 inches long. Cut the wedge slightly thicker than specified, then sand or file one surface to create the taper.

2 **Turn the handle.** Mount the handle stock on a lathe and turn the shape, as shown in the *Handle Layout*. Finish sand the handle on the lathe.

FOR YOUR INFORMATION

Old-time wheelwrights often cut a segment from the rim of a broken wagon wheel to make a mallet head. The wheel rim head was slightly curved, and the faces were cut at a slight angle to each other. This design proved both functional and aesthetically pleasing, and it quickly spread to woodworkers in other trades.

3 **Cut the shape of the head.** Lay out the profile of the head, as shown in the *Side View*, and cut it with a band saw or coping saw. Sand the sawed edges.

4   Drill holes in the head. Lay out the eye for the handle and the holes for the reinforcing dowels on the head. Drill a ¾-inch-diameter hole for the eye and ½-inch-diameter holes for the dowels.

5   Assemble and finish the mallet. With a band saw or a coping saw, cut a ¹⁄₁₆-inch-wide, 1-inch-long slot in the top end of the handle. Glue the reinforcing dowels and the handle in the head. Before the glue dries, turn the handle so the slot runs side to side, as shown in the *Top View*, put a little glue on the wedge, and drive the wedge into the slot as far as it will go. Let the glue dry, then sand the wedge, handle, and the dowels flush with the surfaces of the head.

   Finish sand the assembled mallet. Apply several coats of penetrating finish, let it dry, then wax and buff the surfaces.

MAKING THE CARVER'S MALLET

1   Cut the stock to size. Select a hard, closed-grain wood and cut a turning blank about 3 inches square and 11 inches long.

2   Turn and finish the mallet. Mount the blank on a lathe and turn the shape of the mallet, as shown in the *Carver's Mallet Layout*. Finish sand the mallet

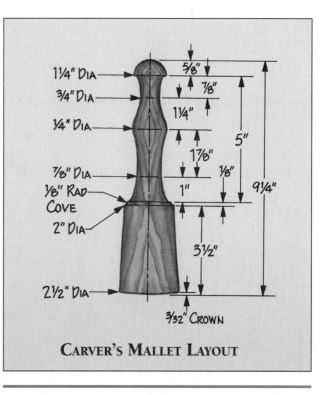

CARVER'S MALLET LAYOUT

on the lathe, except for the ends. Remove the turning, cut away the waste, and finish sand the ends. Apply a penetrating finish, let it dry, and wax and buff the surface.

FLUSH-CUT SAW

The teeth of a *flush-cut saw* are set to one side only, and the blade is mounted with the set facing *up*. This way, the teeth won't scratch a wooden surface when you're cutting dowels, screw plugs, tenons, edge banding, and other protruding wooden parts flush. The blade of the saw shown was cut from an old, worn-out handsaw and then fastened to a wooden handle.

Materials List
(FINISHED DIMENSIONS)

Parts

A. Handle   2″ x 3″ x 8″

Hardware

Saw blade (2″ x 8″ — cut from an
    old handsaw)

#8 x ½″ Flathead wood screws (3)

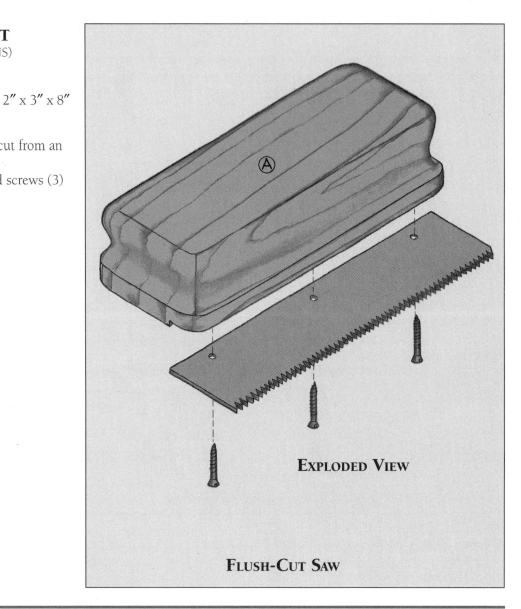

Exploded View

Flush-Cut Saw

Plan of Procedure

1 Cut the handle to size. Select a hard, closed-grain wood for the handle and cut it to the size specified in the Materials List.

2 Shape the handle. Cut a 1-inch-wide round-bottom groove in the edges and the ends of the handle, either by routing the stock with a large core-box bit or by making a cove cut on a table saw. Also round over the top edges of the handle. Using a cabinetmaker's rasp, blend the rounded edges into the round-bottom groove, creating an S-curve, as shown in the *Side View* and *End View*. This will make the handle comfortable to hold.

3 Cut and sharpen the blade. Select an old, worn-out handsaw. (If you don't have one, you can often find them at yard sales and flea markets.) Find a section of the blade that's still fairly straight and cut a 2-inch-wide, 8-inch-long strip from the sawtooth edge. **Note:** Handsaw blades are made from hardened steel, and cutting through one is not an easy task — you will likely use up two or three hacksaw blades in the process. Fine-tooth hacksaw blades (with 24 teeth or more per inch) will cut fastest and last longest. Alternatively, you can rough cut the blade to size with an abrasive wheel in an angle grinder, then grind it to its final size with a bench grinder. Be careful as you're

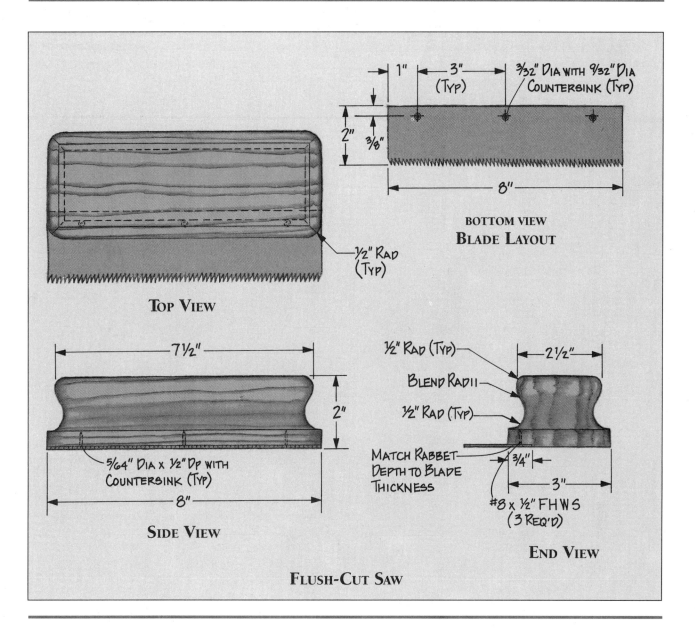

TOP VIEW

BOTTOM VIEW
BLADE LAYOUT

1"
3"
(TYP)
³⁄₃₂" DIA WITH ⁹⁄₃₂" DIA COUNTERSINK (TYP)
2"
³⁄₈"
8"

½" RAD (TYP)

7½"
2"
5⁄64" DIA x ½" DP WITH COUNTERSINK (TYP)
8"

SIDE VIEW

½" RAD (TYP)
BLEND RADII
½" RAD (TYP)
MATCH RABBET DEPTH TO BLADE THICKNESS
2½"
¾"
3"
#8 x ½" FHWS (3 REQ'D)

END VIEW

FLUSH-CUT SAW

grinding not to get the blade too hot or you'll ruin its temper.

Sand or grind the *bottom side* of the blade to remove the set from the teeth that are bent toward the bottom. Do not sand the top side. Joint and sharpen the teeth for crosscuts, as described in "Caring for Saws" on page 33. If you must reset the teeth, set every other tooth toward the top side. Do not set the teeth in between at all.

4 **Mount the blade to the handle.** Using a table-mounted router or a dado cutter, cut a ¾-inch-wide rabbet in the bottom surface of the handle, just deep enough to hold the saw blade. Drill and countersink

³⁄₃₂-inch-diameter holes in the blade, as shown in the *Blade Layout*. (The countersinks must be in the *bottom* surface of the blade.) Use the blade as a template to mark the locations of the ⁵⁄₆₄-inch-diameter, ½-inch-deep pilot holes in the bottom of the handle, and drill them. Fasten the blade to the handle with #8 flathead wood screws. **Note:** The heads of the screws must rest below the surface of the blade, and the set teeth must face *up*.

5 **Finish the saw.** Remove the blade and finish sand the wooden handle. Apply a penetrating finish, let it dry, then wax and buff the surface. Mount the blade back on the handle.

SLIDING BEVEL

A *sliding bevel* copies angles for accurate layouts of tool setups. Most models do not measure angles, but this particular shopmade tool has two rotating bezels — one on each side of the handle — that turn as you change the angle of the blade. Mark one bezel with a protractor scale to help set angles. Leave the other blank so you can mark specific angles on it that you will use for a particular project.

This tool has another useful feature you can't find on commercial models: To quickly set it to 45 degrees, simply rest the butt end of the handle on a flat surface, slide the blade until the mitered end is flat on the same surface, and lock the blade in place.

These two features — rotating bezels and quick-set 45-degree angle — make this handmade bevel much more useful than any you can buy.

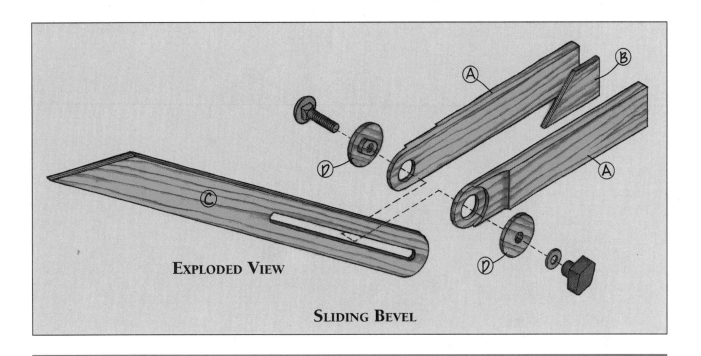

EXPLODED VIEW

SLIDING BEVEL

MATERIALS LIST (FINISHED DIMENSIONS)

Parts

A. Handle halves
   (2) $\frac{3}{8}$" x $1\frac{1}{2}$" x $8\frac{1}{4}$"
B. Spacer* $\frac{1}{8}$" x $1\frac{1}{2}$" x $2\frac{3}{4}$"
C. Blade* $\frac{1}{8}$" x $1\frac{1}{2}$" x $12\frac{1}{8}$"
D. Bezels (2) $1\frac{1}{2}$" dia. x $\frac{5}{16}$"

Make these parts from $\frac{1}{8}$-inch plywood.

Hardware

$\frac{1}{4}$" x $1\frac{1}{4}$" Carriage bolt
$\frac{1}{4}$" Flat washer
$\frac{1}{4}$" T-knob

PLAN OF PROCEDURE

1 Cut the stock to size. Select a hard, closed-grain wood for the handle halves and the bezels. Make the blade and the spacer from $\frac{1}{8}$-inch Baltic birch or Apple-ply plywood. Cut the handle halves, blade, and spacer to the sizes specified in the Materials List. Cut a $\frac{5}{16}$-inch-thick, $1\frac{1}{2}$-inch-wide, 6-inch-long strip to make the bezels.

2 Machine the bezels. Using a table-mounted router, cut $\frac{9}{16}$-inch-wide, $\frac{3}{16}$-inch-deep rabbets in both edges of the bezel stock, leaving a $\frac{3}{8}$-inch-wide tongue down the center of the strip. Cut two pieces $1\frac{1}{2}$ inches square from the strip, then cut another rabbet, $\frac{3}{8}$ inch wide and $\frac{3}{16}$ inch deep, in each end of each piece. The tongue will become a $\frac{3}{8}$-inch-wide, $\frac{3}{4}$-inch-long raised "field" on each piece.

Drill a $\frac{1}{4}$-inch-diameter hole through the center of each field. With a chisel and a file, round the ends of the fields, as shown in the *Bezel Layout*. Sand the square pieces round on a belt sander or a disc sander, using the holes to turn the pieces around a pivot. (*SEE FIGURES 8-1 AND 8-2.*)

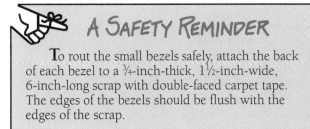

A SAFETY REMINDER

To rout the small bezels safely, attach the back of each bezel to a $\frac{3}{4}$-inch-thick, $1\frac{1}{2}$-inch-wide, 6-inch-long scrap with double-faced carpet tape. The edges of the bezels should be flush with the edges of the scrap.

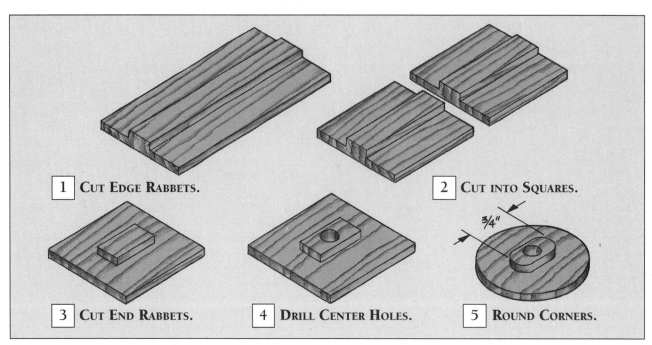

1 | CUT EDGE RABBETS.

2 | CUT INTO SQUARES.

3/4"

3 | CUT END RABBETS.

4 | DRILL CENTER HOLES.

5 | ROUND CORNERS.

8-1 To make the bezels, perform the following operations in order: (1) Cut rabbets in both edges of the stock. (2) Cut the stock into square pieces. (3) Cut rabbets in the ends of the squares. (4) Drill holes through the centers of the squares. (5) Round the square corners. When you do, be careful not to shorten the raised field; it should remain exactly ¾ inch long.

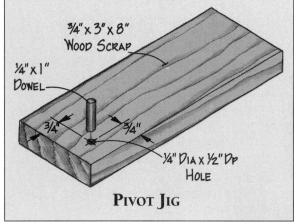

¾" x 3" x 8"
WOOD SCRAP

¼" x 1"
DOWEL

¾"   ¾"

¼" DIA x ½" DP
HOLE

PIVOT JIG

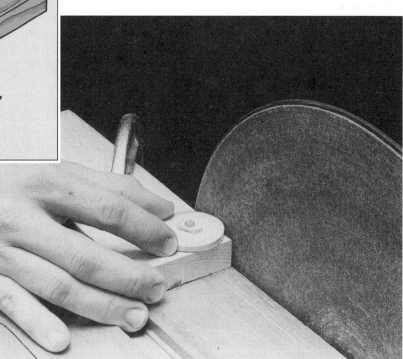

8-2 To sand the bezels round, make this pivot jig and clamp it to the table of a belt sander or disc sander. Position the pivot about 1 inch away from the abrasive. Place each bezel over the pivot, turn on the sander, and rotate the bezel one full revolution to knock off the corners. Turn off the sander, move the jig a little closer to the abrasive, and sand again. Repeat until the bezels are perfectly round.

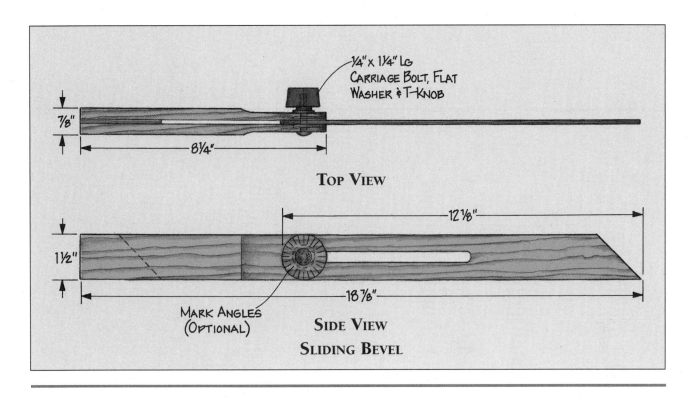

¼" x 1¼" LG
CARRIAGE BOLT, FLAT
WASHER & T-KNOB

7/8"

8¼"

TOP VIEW

12 ⅛"

1½"

18 ⅞"

MARK ANGLES
(OPTIONAL)

SIDE VIEW

SLIDING BEVEL

3 **Machine the handle halves.** Stack the two handle halves face to face and tape them together with double-faced carpet tape. On one half, lay out the location of the ¾-inch-diameter hole, as shown in the *Handle Layout/Side View*. Mark the center of the hole, then drill a ¹⁄₁₆-inch-diameter hole at the mark through *both* halves.

Drill a 1½-inch-diameter, ¼-inch-deep counterbore in each handle half, using the ¹⁄₁₆-inch-diameter hole

to center the bit. Then drill a ¾-inch-diameter hole through both halves, centering the hole in the counterbores.

Using a band saw or a belt sander, thin out the stock, removing ⅛ inch from each handle half in the vicinity of the counterbores, as shown in the *Handle Layout/Top View*. When the stock is thinned out, the counterbores should be ⅛ inch deep — just deep enough to hold the bezels. (*SEE FIGURE 8-3.*)

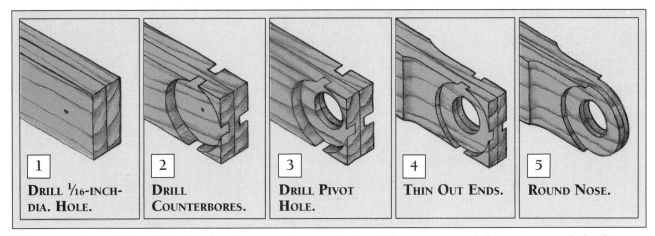

1 DRILL ¹⁄₁₆-INCH-DIA. HOLE.

2 DRILL COUNTERBORES.

3 DRILL PIVOT HOLE.

4 THIN OUT ENDS.

5 ROUND NOSE.

8-3 **To machine the handle halves,** perform the following operations in order: (1) Drill a small hole through both halves to mark the center of the counterbores and pivot holes. (2) Make the counterbores. (3) Drill the pivot hole. (4) Thin out the stock around the counterbores. (5) Finally, round the nose to match the diameter of the bezels.

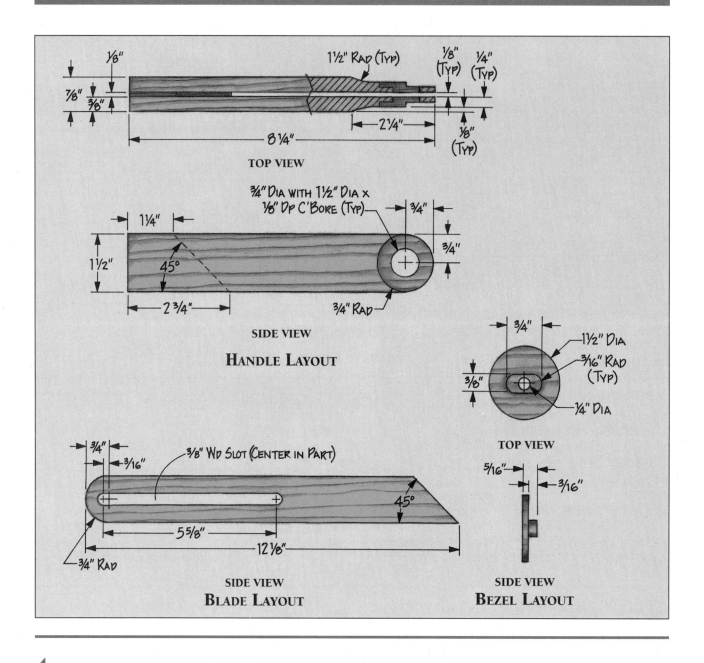

TOP VIEW

¾" DIA WITH 1½" DIA x
⅛" DP C'BORE (TYP)

SIDE VIEW

HANDLE LAYOUT

1½" DIA
3/16" RAD
(TYP)
¼" DIA

TOP VIEW

⅜" WD SLOT (CENTER IN PART)

SIDE VIEW
BLADE LAYOUT

SIDE VIEW
BEZEL LAYOUT

4   Cut and machine the blade and spacer.
Using a table-mounted router, rout a ⅜-inch-wide
slot in the blade, as shown in the *Blade Layout*. Round
one end of the blade and cut a 45-degree angle on
the other. Also cut a 45-degree angle on one end of
the spacer.

5   Assemble and finish the sliding bevel. Glue
the spacer and handle halves together. Before the glue
dries, attach the blade and bezels to the handle
assembly with a carriage bolt, washer, and T-knob —
this will help keep the parts aligned while the glue

sets up. However, be careful not to get any glue on the
blade or the bezels.

After the glue dries, test the action of the blade. It
should turn and slide easily. When you change the
angle of the blade, both bezels should turn with it. If
the blade or the bezels bind, *lightly* sand or file the
binding surfaces until the action is smooth.

Once the sliding bevel is operating properly,
remove the blade and the bezels from the handle.
Sand the handle edges flush, and finish sand all
wooden parts. Apply a penetrating finish, let it dry,
then wax and buff the surfaces. Reattach the blade
and the bezels to the handle.

STRIKING KNIFE

This *striking knife* gives you two choices for marking wood. Use the awl point to scratch the surface when marking with the grain, or use the knife blade to mark across the grain.

MATERIALS LIST
(FINISHED DIMENSIONS)

Parts

A. Handle $^7/_8$" dia. x 6"

Hardware

$^3/_{16}$" Steel rod (5$^1/_2$" long)
$^1/_{16}$" Steel blade ($^5/_8$" x 3")

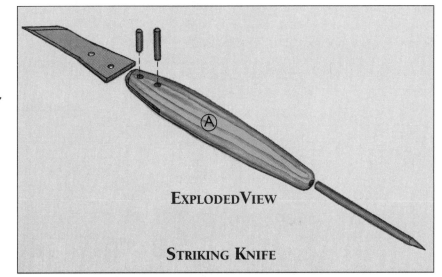

EXPLODED VIEW

STRIKING KNIFE

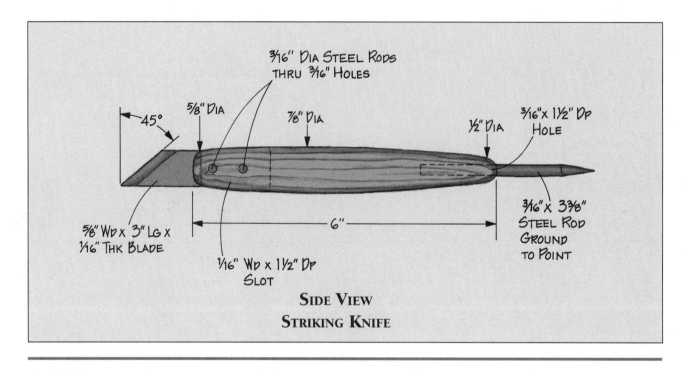

SIDE VIEW
STRIKING KNIFE

PLAN OF PROCEDURE

1 **Cut and machine the handle stock.** Select a hard, closed-grain wood and cut a turning blank about 1 inch square and 8 inches long. Drill a ³⁄₁₆-inch-diameter, 2½-inch-deep hole in one end of the handle, and cut a ¹⁄₁₆-inch-wide, 2½-inch-long slot in the other. Don't worry if the slot seems too long and the hole seems too deep — you'll cut the handle to length later.

2 **Make the metal point and the blade.** From a piece of ¹⁄₁₆-inch-thick tool steel (such as an old handsaw blade), cut a strip ⅝ inch wide and 3 inches long. Miter one end at 45 degrees, and grind a 20-degree bevel in one face of the mitered end.
   Cut three pins from ³⁄₁₆-inch steel rod — one 3⅜ inches long and two ⅞ inch long. Using a grinder or a sander, grind a long, tapered point on one end of the long pin.

A BIT OF ADVICE

Think about how you will use the striking knife before you grind the bevel. Are you right-handed or left-handed? Do you prefer to pull the knife toward you or push it away? Grind the bevel on the side of the blade *opposite* the side that you will likely hold against a straightedge or a square.

3 **Drill mounting holes in the handle and blade.** Insert the blade in the slotted end of the handle stock and drill two ³⁄₁₆-inch-diameter holes through the handle and the blade, as shown in the *Side View*. Remove the blade from the handle.

4 **Turn the handle.** Mount the handle blank on a lathe. To do this without splitting out the slotted end, drill a shallow hole in the end to accept the point of the drive center, and cut a second slot just ¼ inch long, perpendicular to the first. The two slots will hold the drive center spurs. Turn the handle to the shape shown in the *Side View*. Finish sand the handle on the lathe, remove the turning, and cut 1 inch of waste from each end.

5 **Assemble and finish the striking knife.** Insert the blade in the slotted end of the handle and drive the two ⅞-inch-long steel pins through the holes. (If they're not tight in their holes, secure them with epoxy cement.) File the ends of the pins flush with the handle. Fasten the long, pointed pin in the other end of the handle with epoxy.
   Let the cement harden, then do any necessary touch-up sanding to the wooden handle. Apply a penetrating finish, let it dry, then wax and buff the handle. Sharpen the knife blade.

COMBINATION GAUGE

Craftsmen sometimes keep several marking, cutting, and mortising gauges on hand for complex layouts. Marking a tenon, for instance, requires four separate settings, and if you have just one gauge, you must readjust it every time you make a mark. Not only is this a nuisance, it can be inaccurate.

The *combination gauge* shown solves this problem. This single tool combines a marking gauge, a cutting gauge, and two mortising gauges. You can set each of these independently, allowing you to lay out a tenon and other complex joints without having to change settings or keep multiple marking tools on hand.

The tool has two bars that slide through two guides. There is a layout tool at each end of each bar. One bar holds a mortising gauge and a marking gauge, while the other holds a mortising gauge and a cutting gauge. Setting these gauges is slightly different than setting single gauges. Either you must loosen *both* of the knobs that hold a single bar in the guides or you must loosen *both* the knobs that hold a single guide on the bars. Slide the moving parts until the cutting tool or the scratch point is properly positioned in relation to the guides, then tighten the knobs.

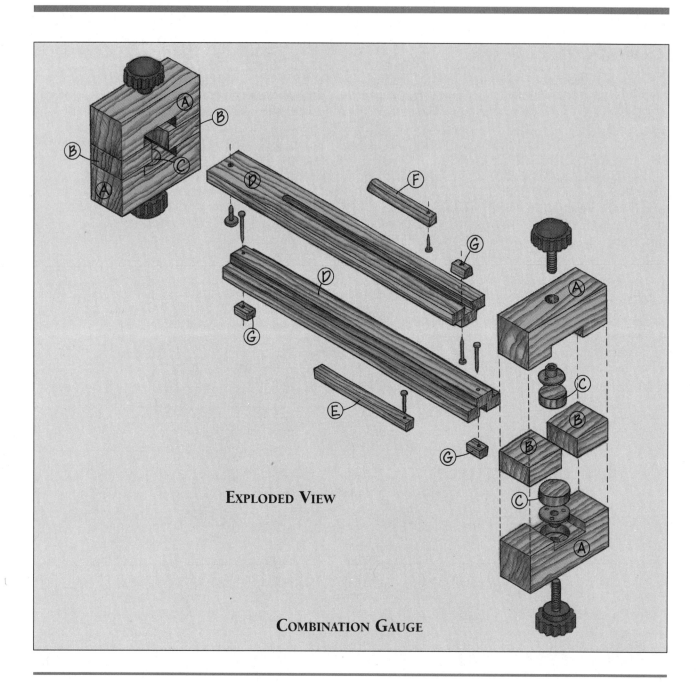

EXPLODED VIEW

COMBINATION GAUGE

MATERIALS LIST (FINISHED DIMENSIONS)

Parts

A. Guides (4)   1″ x 1″ x 2½″
B. Spacers (4)   ½″ x 1″ x 1″
C. Pressure pads (4) ¼″ x ¾″ dia.
D. Bars (2)   ½″ x 1″ x 8″
E. Long slide   ¹³/₆₄″ x ¼″ x 3″
F. Short slide   ¹³/₆₄″ x ¼″ x 2″
G. Dovetail
     plugs (3)   ¹³/₆₄″ x ¼″ x ⅜″

Hardware

⅞″ Knobs with #10 x ⅝″ studs (4)
#10 x ⅜″ T-nuts (4)
1″ Roofing nail
Paneling nails (5)

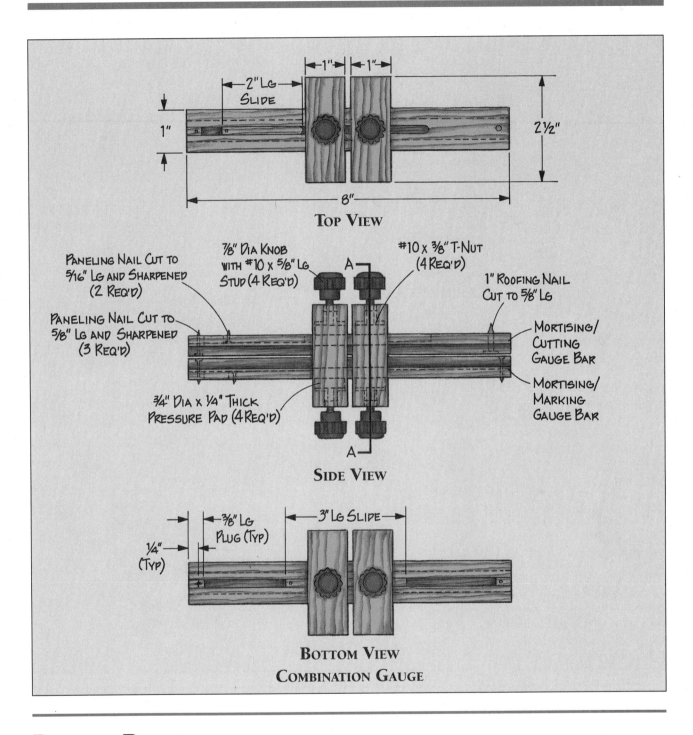

TOP VIEW

2" Lg Slide

1"

1" 1"

2½"

8"

PANELING NAIL CUT TO 5/16" Lg AND SHARPENED (2 REQ'D)

7/8" DIA KNOB WITH #10 x 5/8" Lg STUD (4 REQ'D)

#10 x 3/8" T-NUT (4 REQ'D)

PANELING NAIL CUT TO 5/8" Lg AND SHARPENED (3 REQ'D)

1" ROOFING NAIL CUT TO 5/8" Lg

A

3/4" DIA x 1/4" THICK PRESSURE PAD (4 REQ'D)

MORTISING/ CUTTING GAUGE BAR

MORTISING/ MARKING GAUGE BAR

A

SIDE VIEW

3/8" Lg PLUG (TYP)

3" Lg SLIDE

1/4" (TYP)

BOTTOM VIEW
COMBINATION GAUGE

PLAN OF PROCEDURE

1 Cut the parts to size. Select a hard, closed-grain wood and cut the guides, spacers, and bars to the sizes specified in the Materials List. Cut a ¼-inch-thick, 1-inch-wide, 6-inch-long strip to make the pressure pads, and a ¹³⁄₆₄-inch-thick, 2-inch-wide, 6-inch-long strip to make the slides and plugs. (These larger workpieces will be easier and safer to machine.)

2 Cut the dovetail slots, slides, and plugs. Using a table-mounted router and a ¼-inch dovetail bit, cut a ¼-inch-wide, ³⁄₁₆-inch-deep slot in one face of each bar. Note that the slot on the mortising/cutting gauge bar is blind on one end — it's just 6 inches long. The second slot runs the full length of the mortising/marking gauge bar.

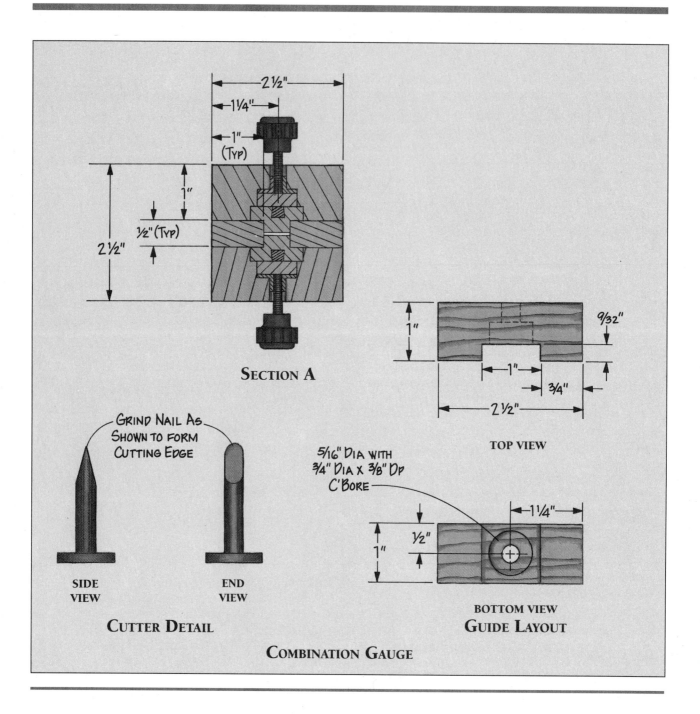

2½"

1¼"

1"
(Typ)

1"

½" (Typ)

2½"

SECTION A

GRIND NAIL AS
SHOWN TO FORM
CUTTING EDGE

SIDE
VIEW

END
VIEW

CUTTER DETAIL

1"

9/32"

1"

3/4"

2½"

TOP VIEW

5/16" DIA WITH
3/4" DIA X 3/8" DP
C'BORE

1¼"

½"

1"

BOTTOM VIEW
GUIDE LAYOUT

COMBINATION GAUGE

From the ¹³⁄₆₄-inch-thick stock, rip ¼-inch-wide strips. As you rip them, bevel the edges to fit the dovetail slots. The strips should slide in the slots easily, without binding. But the fit must not be sloppy — there should be as little play as possible between the sides of the dovetail slots and the beveled edges of the strips. The top surfaces of the strips should protrude ¹⁄₆₄ inch above the bars.

When you have ripped two strips that fit the slots properly, cut them to length to make the long slide,

short slide, and dovetail plugs. Round one end of the short slide to fit the blind end of the slot in the mortising/cutting gauge bar.

3 **Cut the joinery in the guides and the bars.**
Using a table-mounted router or a dado cutter, cut a 1-inch-wide, ⁹⁄₃₂-inch-deep dado in each guide. Also cut a ¼-inch-wide, ⁷⁄₃₂-inch-wide rabbet in each edge of each bar, as shown in the *Mortising/Cutting Gauge Bar Layout/End View.*

4 Assemble the guides and spacers. Drill a ¾-inch-diameter, ⅜-inch-deep counterbore and a ⁵⁄₁₆-inch-diameter hole in the bottom of the dado in each guide, as shown in the *Guide Layout/Bottom View.* Fasten a T-nut in each counterbored hole with epoxy cement. When the epoxy hardens, glue the guides and spacers together, making sure the surfaces are flat and flush with one another.

5 Make the pressure pads. From the ¼-inch-thick stock, cut four ¾-inch-diameter disks using a scroll saw or a coping saw. Sand the sawed edges so the pads fit loosely inside the guide counterbores.

TRY THIS TRICK

To sand the tiny pads without sanding your fingers, attach them to the end of a dowel with carpet tape.

6 Drill the holes for the cutter and scratch points. In the blind end of the mortising/cutting gauge bar, drill a ⁹⁄₆₄-inch-diameter hole with a ⅜-inch-diameter, ¹⁄₁₆-inch-deep counterbore. Insert the plugs in the dovetail slots in the bars. Position the plugs flush with the ends of the slots, and drill ¹⁄₁₆-inch-diameter holes with ⅛-inch-diameter, ¹⁄₁₆-inch-deep counterbores through the bars and the plugs, as

shown in the *Side View, Bottom View,* and *Mortising/Cutting Gauge Bar Layout.* Also drill ¹⁄₁₆-inch-diameter holes with ⅛-inch-diameter, ¹⁄₁₆-inch-deep counterbores in the ends of the slides. (SEE FIGURE 8-4.)

7 Finish and assemble the gauge. Temporarily assemble the combination gauge *without* the cutter or the scratch points. Screw the knobs into the guides and place the pressure pads in the counterbores. Insert the slides in the bars, then insert the bars in the guides. Test the action — the bars should slide through the guides smoothly. When you tighten the knobs, they should lock both the bars and the slides in place.

When you're satisfied that the parts of the gauge all work together properly, take them apart and remove the knobs. Finish sand the wooden parts and apply a penetrating finish. Let it dry, then wax and buff all wooden surfaces.

Cut three paneling nails and a roofing nail ⅝ inch long and two more paneling nails ⁵⁄₁₆ inch long. Drive the roofing nail into the counterbored hole in the blind end of the mortising/cutting gauge bar. The head of the nail must rest in the counterbore, flush with or slightly below the wood surface. Position a plug in one end of the mortising/marking gauge bar, and drive one of the ⅝-inch-long paneling nails through the bar and plug. Again, the head must rest in the counterbore.

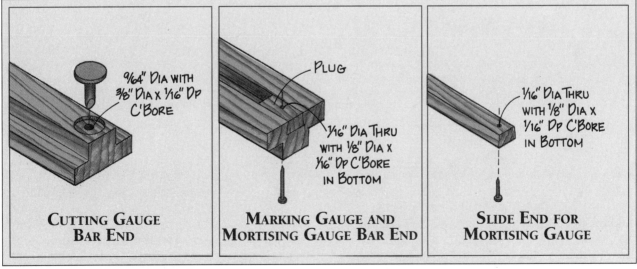

8-4 How you drill the ends of the bars and the slides depends on the layout tool that you will mount in it. Wherever you mount a scratch point, drill a ¹⁄₁₆-inch-diameter hole with a ⅛-inch-diameter, ¹⁄₁₆-inch-deep counterbore. Wherever you mount a cutter, drill a ⁹⁄₆₄-inch-diameter hole with a ⅜-inch-diameter, ¹⁄₁₆-inch-deep counterbore.

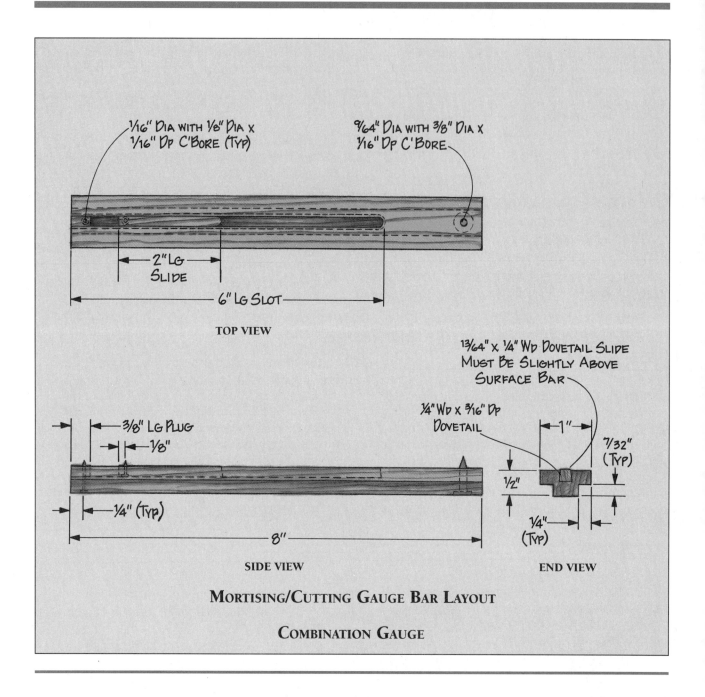

TOP VIEW

SIDE VIEW   **END VIEW**

MORTISING/CUTTING GAUGE BAR LAYOUT

COMBINATION GAUGE

Screw the knobs in the guides and insert the pressure pads in the counterbores. Slide the bars into the guides so the roofing nail and the paneling nail are on the same side. Drive the 5/16-inch-long paneling nails into the holes in the ends of the slides. Insert the short slide (round end first) into the blind dovetail slot in the mortising/cutting gauge bar, and insert the long slide into the through slot in the mortising/ marking gauge bar.

Slide one bar through the guides so the end with the blind dovetail slot protrudes about 1 inch past the other bar. Insert a plug in the slot and drive a 5/8-inch-long paneling nail through the bar and the plug. Repeat for the other bar. **Note:** Don't glue the plugs in the slots; the nails will hold them in place. You want to be able to remove them in the event you need to disassemble the combination gauge to repair it.

File sharp, tapering points on the ends of the paneling nails, making sure they all protrude *precisely* the same distance above the bars. File a knife-like cutting edge on the roofing nail, as shown in the *Cutter Detail.*

USING THE COMBINATION GAUGE

You can use the four layout tools on the gauge singly or in combinations of two or three, depending on the work you have to do. Select the marking gauge when you need to scratch a single line parallel to an edge in the *same direction* as the wood grain. To cut a line parallel to an end and *across* the grain, choose the cutting gauge. To scratch two parallel lines, use one of the mortising gauges.

1 **To set just one of the tools,** determine which bar it's on. Loosen the two knobs that hold that bar in the guides (one knob on each guide), then slide the bar through the guides until the cutter or the scratch point is the desired distance from the guide. If you're setting a mortising gauge, first slide the bar to set the distance for the *far* point (the scratch point farthest from the guide), then position the slide to set the *near* point. Tighten both knobs — the pads will hold both the bars and the slides in place.

2 **As an alternative, you could** loosen both knobs on a single guide. Slide the guide along the bars until it's the desired distance from the cutter or scratch point. If necessary, adjust the position of the slide. Then tighten the knobs.

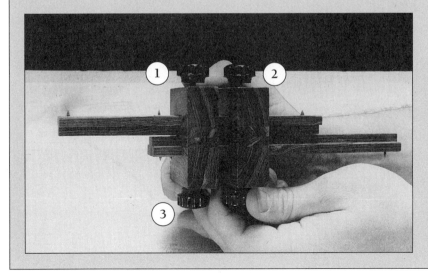

3 **To set two or three tools in** combination, you must loosen at least three and possibly all four knobs to move both the guides and the bars. Select the tools you want to use. If two tools lie along the same bar, set those *first*, tightening the knobs as you adjust each cutter or scratch point. Set the tool that resides on the bar with the unused tool *last*, then tighten all the knobs. **Note:** The most tools you can use at any one time is three; you won't be able to set the fourth tool without disturbing one of the others.

INDEX

Note: Page references in *italic* indicate photographs or illustrations.
Boldface references indicate charts or tables.

WOODWORKING GLOSSARY

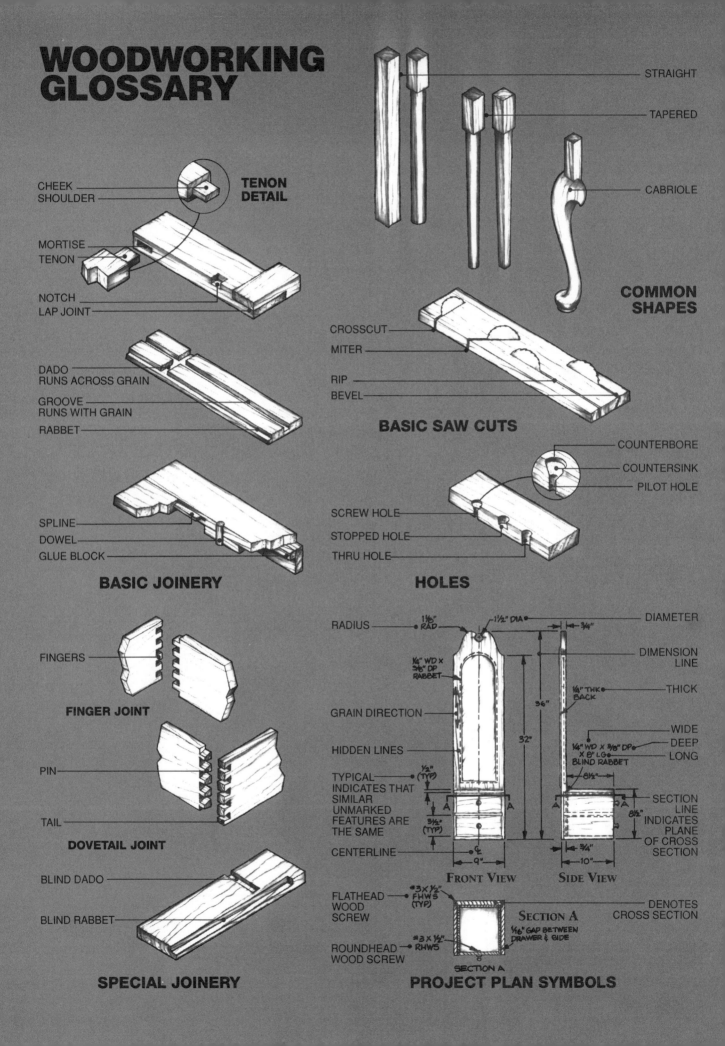

TENON DETAIL
- CHEEK
- SHOULDER
- MORTISE
- TENON
- NOTCH
- LAP JOINT

COMMON SHAPES
- STRAIGHT
- TAPERED
- CABRIOLE

BASIC JOINERY
- DADO RUNS ACROSS GRAIN
- GROOVE RUNS WITH GRAIN
- RABBET
- SPLINE
- DOWEL
- GLUE BLOCK

BASIC SAW CUTS
- CROSSCUT
- MITER
- RIP
- BEVEL

HOLES
- COUNTERBORE
- COUNTERSINK
- PILOT HOLE
- SCREW HOLE
- STOPPED HOLE
- THRU HOLE

FINGER JOINT
- FINGERS

DOVETAIL JOINT
- PIN
- TAIL

SPECIAL JOINERY
- BLIND DADO
- BLIND RABBET

PROJECT PLAN SYMBOLS
- RADIUS — 1⅛" RAD
- 1½" DIA — DIAMETER
- ¾" — DIMENSION LINE
- ¼" WD x ⅜" DP RABBET
- GRAIN DIRECTION
- 36"
- 32"
- ¼" THK BACK — THICK
- ¼" WD x ⅜" DP X 8" LG BLIND RABBET — WIDE / DEEP / LONG
- HIDDEN LINES
- TYPICAL INDICATES THAT SIMILAR UNMARKED FEATURES ARE THE SAME — ½" (TYP)
- 3½" (TYP)
- 8½"
- SECTION LINE INDICATES PLANE OF CROSS SECTION
- CENTERLINE — 9"
- ¾"
- 10"
- FRONT VIEW
- SIDE VIEW
- FLATHEAD WOOD SCREW — #3 X ½" FHWS (TYP)
- ROUNDHEAD WOOD SCREW — #3 X ½" RHWS
- ⅟₁₆" GAP BETWEEN DRAWER & SIDE
- SECTION A
- DENOTES CROSS SECTION